Appcelerator Titanium Smartphone App Development Cookbook

Over 80 recipes for creating native mobile applications specifically for iPhone and Android smartphones – no Objective-C or Java required

Boydlee Pollentine

BIRMINGHAM - MUMBAI

Appcelerator Titanium Smartphone
App Development Cookbook

First published: December 2011

Production Reference: 1091211

Published by Packt Publishing Ltd.
Livery Place
35 Livery Street
Birmingham B3 2PB, UK.

ISBN 978-1-84951-396-8

www.packtpub.com

Cover Image by Asher Wishkerman (wishkerman@hotmail.com)

Credits

Author

Boydlee Pollentine

Reviewers

Imraan Jhetam

Julian Lynch

Peter Puglisi

Acquisition Editor

Chaitanya Apte

Development Editor

Hyacintha D'Souza

Technical Editors

Veronica Fernandes

Ajay Shankar

Sonali Tharwani

Copy Editor

Neha Shetty

Laxmi Subramanian

Project Coordinator

Kushal Bhardwaj

Proofreader

Joel T. Johnson

Indexer

Hemangini Bari

Tejal Daruwale

Production Coordinator

Aparna Bhagat

Cover Work

Aparna Bhagat

About the Author

Boydlee Pollentine is a keen mobile developer who has created numerous apps for the iTunes and Android stores and a number of indie games. He is passionate about mobile development, and in particular the Appcelerator Titanium platform. He is both a Titanium Certified Application developer and a member of the Titans evangelist group.

He has been a software engineer and programmer for the last 10 years, primarily focusing on web technologies and Microsoft's .NET platform. During this time, he has worked for numerous small and large organizations, including a number of Australian Federal Government departments, state departments, banks, and media organizations.

He currently lives in London and works as a freelance Titanium developer and runs a small blog dedicated to mobile development at `http://boydlee.com`.

I'd like to thank everyone on the Appcelerator forums, Twitter, and the Web, who have helped to contribute and make the great Titanium community what it is today.

About the Reviewers

Imraan Jhetam is a medical doctor and entrepreneur living in England with equal love for both medical law and technology. He earned his Medical Degree from the University of Natal in 1983, his MBA from the University of Witwatersrand, and a Masters of Law Degree from Cardiff University.

He has been fascinated by computers since his youth and has taught himself the basics of programming during his university years. He has been writing programs since the mid 1970's in various languages and for different platforms, and has fond memories of his first Apple IIe with its then impressive 64 KB RAM.

When he is not busy seeing patients or writing medico-legal reports, he spends his time developing applications. He has developed i-MAGiNE, a Magazine Type Pictorial RSS feed reader written using the incredible Titanium Studio tools that is now in the Apple App Store. He was also the third prize winner at the first Codestrong Hackathon with two e-payment apps "PayBill" and "PayPad". These also included social media, geo-location, photos, and bar-codes, and which were developed in a restricted and short time using Appcelerator Titanium Studio.

You can contact Imraan via www.i-magine.mobi or via Twitter @The__i.

Julian Lynch is an Information Systems developer with a web development-focused background. He has been involved in application development for corporate environments including government, private, and public companies.

Peter Puglisi is a freelance developer and consultant based in Brisbane, Australia. He has over 20 years of software engineering experience and has worked on both small and large scale projects in the transport, defense, mining, agricultural, pharmaceutical, and financial industries.

More recently, he has been developing iPhone and iPad apps for his successful and growing mobile development business, Bright Light Apps.

He holds a Bachelor of Electrical Engineering degree from James Cook University and a Post Graduate Diploma in Applied Computing from Central Queensland University. He lives in Brisbane with his wife Sarina, and children, Anthony and Christina.

He can be reached via LinkedIn at `http://www.linkedin.com/in/peterpuglisi`.

www.PacktPub.com

Support files, eBooks, discount offers and more

You might want to visit www.PacktPub.com for support files and downloads related to your book.

Did you know that Packt offers eBook versions of every book published, with PDF and ePub files available? You can upgrade to the eBook version at www.PacktPub.com and as a print book customer, you are entitled to a discount on the eBook copy. Get in touch with us at service@packtpub.com for more details.

At www.PacktPub.com, you can also read a collection of free technical articles, sign up for a range of free newsletters and receive exclusive discounts and offers on Packt books and eBooks.

http://PacktLib.PacktPub.com

Do you need instant solutions to your IT questions? PacktLib is Packt's online digital book library. Here, you can access, read and search across Packt's entire library of books.

Why Subscribe?

- ► Fully searchable across every book published by Packt
- ► Copy and paste, print and bookmark content
- ► On demand and accessible via web browser

Free Access for Packt account holders

If you have an account with Packt at www.PacktPub.com, you can use this to access PacktLib today and view nine entirely free books. Simply use your login credentials for immediate access.

Table of Contents

Preface

Not so long ago, creating a mobile application and getting it published was difficult, costly, and, for most developers, commercially unviable. Flash forward a number of years to the introduction of the iPhone and App Store, and suddenly there was a way where anyone who could write a code in Apple's Objective-C language, and had a healthy understanding of provisioning certificates for the Mac, could write a smartphone application and distribute it worldwide with minimal amount of fuss and very little red tape. During the last decade, many of us in the web development community have moved away from archaic C-based languages, and have squarely focused much of our programming knowledge on JavaScript, that ubiquitous little language that despite all its shortcomings has gained momentum and was commonplace both on and off the Web.

Shortly after that, we began to see a number of "alternative" platforms emerge which promised developers the ability to build mobile applications without the hassle of re-skilling in Objective-C, or in the case of Android, in Java. Among these was a newcomer called Titanium Mobile, which held the promise of allowing native applications to be built using only JavaScript, and the ability to make those applications cross-platform (across both iOS and Android). As of December 2011, Appcelerator's Titanium Mobile boasts over 1.5 million active developers and has released 30,000 applications in the marketplace. It has the backing of major players such as eBay and powers some of the world's most popular apps, including Wunderlist, eBay Mobile, and GetGlue. There is support for Blackberry and the mobile web. It also has the ability to build cross-platform games using popular engines such as OpenGL and Box2D. It even has its own Mobile Marketplace, where developers can sell and distribute their Titanium modules to the rest of the community.

In this book, we'll cover all of the aspects of building your mobile applications in Titanium Mobile, from layout to maps and GPS, all the way through social media integration and accessing your device's input hardware, including the camera and microphone. Each "recipe" described within is a self-contained lesson. You may pick and choose which areas you wish to read and use it as a reference. Alternatively, you can follow along each recipe in succession through most chapters and build a small app from start to finish. We'll also go through how to extend your applications using custom modules, and how to package them for distribution and sale in both the iTunes App Store and the Android Marketplace.

What this book covers

In *Chapter 1, Building Apps using Native UI Components*, we'll begin our journey into Titanium Mobile by understanding the basics of layout and creating controls, before moving onto tabbed interfaces, web views, and how to add and open multiple windows.

In *Chapter 2, Working with Local and Remote Data Sources,* we are going to build ourselves a mini-app that reads data from the Web using HTTP requests, and we'll see how to parse and iterate data in both XML and JSON formats. We'll also see how to store and retrieve data locally using an SQLite database and some basic SQL queries.

In *Chapter 3, Integrating Google Maps and GPS,* we'll add a MapView to your application and interact with it using annotations, geo-coding and events that track the user's location. We'll also go through the basics of adding routes and using your device's inbuilt compass to track our heading.

In *Chapter 4, Enhancing your Apps with Audio, Video, and the Camera,* we'll see how to interact with your device's media features using Titanium, including the camera, photo gallery, and audio recorder.

In *Chapter 5, Connecting your Apps with Social Media and E-mail,* we're going to see how to leverage Titanium and integrate it with Facebook, Twitter, and the e-mail capabilities of your mobiles devices. We'll also go through setting up a Facebook application and give you a brief introduction to the world of OAuth.

In *Chapter 6, Getting to Grips with Events and Properties,* we'll briefly run through how properties work in Titanium, and how you can get and set global variables in your app. We'll also explain how event listeners and handlers work and how to fire events, both from your controls and custom events from anywhere in your application.

In *Chapter 7, Creating Animations, Transformations and Understanding Drag-and-drop*, we'll show you how to create animations, and how to transform your objects using 2D and 3D matrices in Titanium. We will also run through dragging and dropping controls and capturing screenshots using the inbuilt "toImage" functionality.

In *Chapter 8, Interacting with Native Phone Applications and APIs*, we will discover how to interact with native device APIs, such as the device's contacts and calendar. We'll also discover how to use local notifications and background services.

In *Chapter 9, Integrating your Apps with External Services*, we'll dive deeper into OAuth and HTTP authentication, and also show you how to connect to external APIs, such as Yahoo! YQL and Foursquare. We will also run through the set up and integration of push notifications into your Titanium apps.

In *Chapter 10, Extending your Apps with Custom Modules*, we will see how you can extend the native functionality in Titanium and add your own custom, native modules using Objective-C and Xcode. We'll run through a sample module from start to finish in Xcode for creating short URLs using the Bit.ly service.

In *Chapter 11*, *Platform Differences, Device Information, and Quirks*, we'll take a look at how to use Titanium to find out information about the device, including important features such as making phone calls, checking the memory, and checking the remaining allocation of the battery. We will also go through screen orientations and how to code differences between the iOS and Android platforms.

In *Chapter 12*, *Preparing your App for Distribution and Getting it Published*, we will see how to prepare and package your applications for distribution and sale to the iTunes App Store and Android Marketplaces, along with a background into how to set up and provision your apps correctly with provisioning profiles and development certificates.

What you need for this book

You will need a Mac running Xcode (the latest version, available at `http://developer.apple.com`) and the Titanium Studio software (available at `www.appcelerator.com`). You must use a Mac, as all instructions are based on it (Unix) because of the iPhone. Using a PC is not recommended or supported in any way for the Apple iPhone.

Who this book is for

This book is essential for any developer who possesses some JavaScript or web development knowledge and wishes to take a leap into building native applications for both the iPhone and Android. No knowledge of Objective-C or Java is required.

Conventions

In this book, you will find a number of styles of text that distinguish between different kinds of information. Here are some examples of these styles, and an explanation of their meaning.

Code words in text are shown as follows: "First, open your `app.js` file, and two more JavaScript files called `recipes.js` and `favorites.js`"

A block of code is set as follows:

```
//add an image to the left of the annotation
var leftImage = Titanium.UI.createImageView({
  image: 'images/start.png',
  width: 25,
  height: 25
});
annotation.leftView = leftImage;

//add the start button
var startButton = 'images/startbutton.png';
annotation.rightButton = startButton;

mapview.addAnnotation(annotation);
```

Any command-line input or output is written as follows:

```
cd /<path to your android sdk>/tools
```

New terms and **important words** are shown in bold. Words that you see on the screen, in menus or dialog boxes for example, appear in the text like this: "Once you are logged in, click on **New Project**, and the details window for creating a new project will appear."

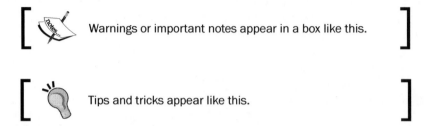

Warnings or important notes appear in a box like this.

Tips and tricks appear like this.

Reader feedback

Feedback from our readers is always welcome. Let us know what you think about this book—what you liked or may have disliked. Reader feedback is important for us to develop titles that you really get the most out of.

To send us general feedback, simply send an e-mail to feedback@packtpub.com, and mention the book title via the subject of your message.

If there is a book that you need and would like to see us publish, please send us a note in the **SUGGEST A TITLE** form on www.packtpub.com or e-mail suggest@packtpub.com.

If there is a topic that you have expertise in and you are interested in either writing or contributing to a book, see our author guide on www.packtpub.com/authors.

Customer support

Now that you are the proud owner of a Packt book, we have a number of things to help you to get the most from your purchase.

Downloading the example code

You can download the example code files for all Packt books you have purchased from your account at http://www.PacktPub.com. If you purchased this book elsewhere, you can visit http://www.PacktPub.com/support and register to have the files e-mailed directly to you.

Errata

Although we have taken every care to ensure the accuracy of our content, mistakes do happen. If you find a mistake in one of our books—maybe a mistake in the text or the code—we would be grateful if you would report this to us. By doing so, you can save other readers from frustration and help us improve subsequent versions of this book. If you find any errata, please report them by visiting http://www.packtpub.com/support, selecting your book, clicking on the **errata submission form** link, and entering the details of your errata. Once your errata are verified, your submission will be accepted and the errata will be uploaded on our website, or added to any list of existing errata, under the Errata section of that title. Any existing errata can be viewed by selecting your title from http://www.packtpub.com/support.

Piracy

Piracy of copyright material on the Internet is an ongoing problem across all media. At Packt, we take the protection of our copyright and licenses very seriously. If you come across any illegal copies of our works, in any form, on the Internet, please provide us with the location address or website name immediately so that we can pursue a remedy.

Please contact us at copyright@packtpub.com with a link to the suspected pirated material.

We appreciate your help in protecting our authors, and our ability to bring you valuable content.

Questions

You can contact us at questions@packtpub.com if you are having a problem with any aspect of the book, and we will do our best to address it.

1
Building Apps using Native UI Components

In this chapter, we will cover:

- ▶ Building with Windows and Views
- ▶ Adding a TabGroup to your app
- ▶ Creating and formatting Labels
- ▶ Creating TextFields for user input
- ▶ Working with keyboards and keyboard toolbars
- ▶ Enhancing your App with Sliders and Switches
- ▶ Passing custom variables between windows
- ▶ Creating buttons and capturing click events
- ▶ Informing your users with dialogs and alerts
- ▶ Creating charts using Raphael JS

Introduction

The ability to create user-friendly layouts with rich, intuitive controls is an important factor in successful app design. With mobile apps and their minimal screen real estate, this becomes even more important. Titanium leverages a huge amount of native controls found in both the iPhone/iPod Touch and Android platforms, allowing the developer to create apps just as rich in functionality as those created by native language developers.

How does this compare to the mobile web? When it comes to HTML/CSS only mobile apps, savvy users can definitely tell the difference in comparison to a platform like Titanium, which allows you to use platform-specific conventions and access your iPhone or Android device's latest and greatest features. An application written in Titanium feels and operates like a native app since essentially all of the UI components are native. This means crisp, responsive UI components utilizing the full capabilities and power of your device.

Most other books at this point would start explaining the fundamental principles of Titanium and maybe give you a rundown on the architecture and expand on the required syntax.

Yawn...

We're not going to do that. Instead, we will be jumping straight into the fun stuff, building your user interface and making a real-world app! In this chapter, you'll learn:

- How to build an app using `Windows` and `Views`, and understanding the differences between the two

- Putting together a UI using all of the common components, including `TextFields`, `Labels` and `Switches`

- Just how similar Titanium component properties are to CSS when formatting your UI

You can pick and choose any recipe from the chapter if you want since each one is a self-contained example that will explain a specific component or process. Alternatively, you can follow each chapter from beginning to end to put together a real-world app for calculating loan repayments which we will call **LoanCalc** from here on in.

Complete source code for this entire chapter can be found in the `/Chapter 1/LoanCalc` folder.

Building with Windows and Views

We are going to start off with the very building blocks of all Titanium applications, Windows and Views. By the end of this recipe you will understand how to implement a Window and add Views to it, as well as understand the fundamental difference between the two, which is not as obvious as it may seem at first glance.

If you are intending to follow the entire chapter and build the LoanCalc app, then pay careful attention to the first few steps of this chapter, as you will need to perform these steps again for each subsequent app in the book.

We are assuming that you have already downloaded and installed Titanium Studio and either Apple XCode with the iOS SDK or Google's Android SDK, or both. If not, you can follow along with the installation process via the online tutorial at `http://boydlee.com/titanium-appcelerator-cookbook/setup`.

Getting ready

To follow this recipe you will need Titanium Studio installed. We are using version 1.0.7, which is the latest version at the time of writing. Additionally, you will also need either the iOS SDK with XCode or the Google Android SDK installed. All of our examples generally work on either platform unless specified explicitly at the start of a chapter. You will also need an IDE to write your code. Any IDE including Notepad, TextMate, Dashcode, Eclipse, and so on, can be used. However, since June 2011, Appcelerator has been providing its own IDE called "Titanium Studio", which is based on Aptana. Titanium Studio allows developers to build, test, and deploy iOS, Android, Blackberry, and mobile web apps from within a single development environment. All of the recipes within this book are based on the assumption that you are using the Titanium Studio product, which can be downloaded for free from `https://my.appcelerator.com/auth/signup/offer/community`.

To prepare for this recipe, open Titanium Studio and log in if you have not already done so. If you need to register a new account, you can do so for free directly from within the application. Once you are logged in, click on **File | New | New Titanium Mobile Project**, and the details window for creating a new project will appear. Enter in LoanCalc the name of the app, and fill in the rest of the details with your own information as shown in the following screenshot. You can also uncheck the **"iPad"** option, as we will only be building our application for the iPhone and Android platforms.

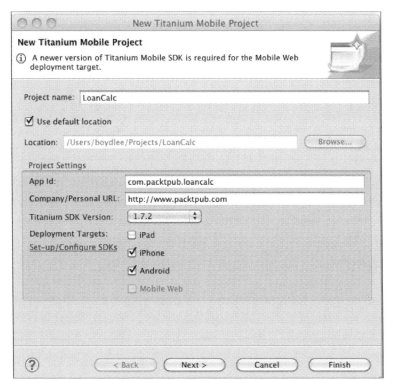

Pay attention to the app identifier, which is written normally in reverse domain notation (that is, `com.packtpub.loancalc`). This identifier cannot be easily changed after the project is created and you will need to match it exactly when creating provisioning profiles for distributing your apps later on.

Complete source code for this recipe can be found in the `/Chapter 1/Recipe 1` folder.

How to do it...

First, open the `app.js` file in Titanium Studio. If this is a new project, by default Titanium Studio creates a sample app containing a couple of Windows inside of a `TabGroup` which is certainly useful but we will cover TabGroups in a later recipe, so go ahead and remove all of the generated code. Now let's create a Window object to which we will add a View object. This View object will hold all of our controls, such as TextFields and Labels.

In addition to creating our base Window and View, we will also create an `ImageView` component to display our app logo before adding it to our View (you can get the image we used from the source code for chapter).

Finally, we'll call the `open()` method on the `Window` to launch it:

```
//create the window
var win1 = Titanium.UI.createWindow({
  width: 320,
  height: 480,
  top: 0,
  left: 0,
  backgroundImage: 'background.png'
});

//create the view, this will hold all of our UI controls
//note the height of this view is the height of the window //minus
40px for the status bar and padding
var view = Titanium.UI.createView({
  width: 300,
  height: win1.height - 40,
  left: 10,
  top: 10,
  backgroundColor: '#fff',
  borderRadius: 5
});

//we will give the logo a left margin so it centers neatly //within
our view
var _logoMarginLeft = (view.width - 253) / 2;

//now let's add our logo to an imageview and add that to our //view
object
```

```
var logo = Titanium.UI.createImageView({
  image: 'logo.png',
  width: 253,
  height: 96,
  left: _logoMarginLeft,
  top: 0
});
view.add(logo);

//add the view to our window
win1.add(view);

//finally, open the window to launch the app
win1.open();
```

Downloading the example code

You can download the example code files for all Packt books you have purchased from your account at `http://www.PacktPub.com`. If you purchased this book elsewhere, you can visit `http://www.PacktPub.com/support` and register to have the files e-mailed directly to you.

How it works...

Firstly, it's important to explain the differences between `Windows` and `Views` as there are a few fundamental differences that may influence your decision on using one compared to the other. Unlike Views, Windows have some additional abilities including an `open()` and `close()` method. If you come from a desktop development background, you can imagine a Window as the equivalent of a form or screen. If you prefer web analogies, then a Window is more like a page whereas Views are more like a Div. In addition to these methods, Windows also have display properties such as `fullscreen` and `modal` which are not available in Views. You will also notice that when creating a new object the `create` keyword pops up, that is `Titanium.UI.createView()`. This naming convention is used consistently throughout the Titanium API, and almost all components are instantiated this way.

Windows and Views can be thought of as the building blocks of your Titanium application. All of your UI components are added to either a Window, or a View, which is a child of a Window. There are a number of formatting options available for both of these objects, the properties and syntax of which will be very familiar to anyone who has used CSS in the past. Font, Color, BorderWidth, BorderRadius, Width, Height, Top, and Left are all properties that function exactly the same way as you would expect them to in CSS and apply to Windows and almost all Views.

It's important to note that your app requires at least one Window to function and that Window must be called from within your entry point which is the app.js file.

You may have also noticed that we sometimes instantiated objects or called methods using `Titanium.UI.createXXX`, and at other times used `Ti.UI.createXXX`. Using "Ti" is simply a short-hand namespace designed to save your time during coding, and will execute your code in exactly the same manner as the full "Titanium" namespace does.

Adding a TabGroup to your app

TabGroups are one of the most commonly used UI elements and form the basis of the layout for many iPhone and Android apps on the market today. The TabGroup consists of a sectioned set of tabs each containing an individual window, which in turn contains a navigation bar and title. On the iPhone, these tabs appear in a horizontal list on the bottom of the screen. On Android devices, by default, they appear as 'upside-down' tabs at the top of the screen, as shown in the next screenshot:

Getting ready

The complete source code for this recipe can be found in the /Chapter 1/Recipe 2 folder.

How to do it...

We are going to create two separate Windows—one of these will be defined in-line and the other Window will be loaded from an external JavaScript file called window2.js. Before writing any code, create a new JavaScript file called window2.js and save it to your Resources directory—the same folder where your app.js currently resides.

If you have been following along with the LoanCalc app so far, then delete the current code we created and replace it with the source below:

```
//create tab group
var tabGroup = Ti.UI.createTabGroup();

//create the window
var win1 = Titanium.UI.createWindow({
  width: 320,
  height: 480,
  top: 0,
  left: 0,
  backgroundImage: 'background.png',
  title: 'Loan Calculator',
  barImage: 'navbar.png'
});

//create the view, this will hold all of our UI controls
//note the height of this view is the height of the window //minus
134px for the status bar and padding and adjusted for //navbar
var view = Titanium.UI.createView({
  width: 300,
  height: win1.height - 134,
  left: 10,
  top: 10,
  backgroundColor: '#fff',
  borderRadius: 5
});

//we will give the logo a left margin so it centers neatly //within
our view
var _logoMarginLeft = (view.width - 253) / 2;

//now let's add our logo to an imageview and add that to our //view
object
var logo = Titanium.UI.createImageView({
  image: 'logo.png',
  width: 253,
  height: 96,
  left: _logoMarginLeft,
  top: 0
});
view.add(logo);

//add the view to our window
win1.add(view);
```

```
//add the first tab and attach our window object (win1) to it
var tab1 = Ti.UI.createTab({
    icon:'icon_calculator.png',
    title:'Calculate',

    window: win1
});

//create the second window for settings tab
var win2 = Titanium.UI.createWindow({
  width: 320,
  height: 480,
  top: 0,
  left: 0,
  backgroundImage: 'background.png',
  url: 'window2.js',
  title: 'Settings',
  barImage: 'navbar.png'
});

//add the second tab and attach our external window object //(win2 /
window2.js) to it
var tab2 = Ti.UI.createTab({
    icon:'icon_settings.png',
    title:'Settings',
    window: win2
});

//now add the tabs to our tabGroup object
tabGroup.addTab(tab1);
tabGroup.addTab(tab2);

//finally, open the tabgroup to launch the app
tabGroup.open();
```

How it works...

Logically, it is important to realize that the TabGroup, when used, is the root of the application and cannot be included from any other UI component. Each Tab within the TabGroup is essentially a wrapper for a single Window that can either be defined in-line or by providing the location of an external JavaScript file using the url property. These Windows are loaded only when that Tab gains focus for the first time, normally via the user tapping the **Tab** icon to gain focus to that particular Window.

The **Tab** icon is loaded from an image file, generally a PNG, but it's important to note that in both Android and the iPhone, all icons will be rendered in greyscale with alpha transparency—any color information will be discarded when you run the application.

There's more...

Apple can be particularly picky when it comes to using icons in your apps. Whenever a standard icon has been defined by Apple (such as the gears icon for *settings*) you should use the same.

A great set of additional 200 free tab bar icons are available at: `http://glyphish.com`.

Creating and formatting Labels

Whether it's for presenting text content to the screen, identifying an input field, or displaying data within a TableRow, Labels are one of the cornerstone UI elements that you'll find yourself using all of the time with Titanium. Through them, you will display the majority of your information to the user, so it is important to know how to create and format them properly.

In this recipe we will create three different labels, one for each input component that we will be adding to our app later on. Using these examples, we will explain how to position your label, give it a text value, and format it.

Getting ready

The complete source code for this recipe can be found in the `/Chapter 1/Recipe 3` folder.

How to do it...

Open up your `app.js` file and begin by putting the following two variables at the top of your code file, directly under the TabGroup creation declaration. These are going to be the default values for our interest rate and loan length for the app:

```
//application variables
var numberMonths = 36; //loan length
var interestRate = 6.0; //interest rate
```

Let's create labels to identify the input fields we will be implementing later on. Type in the following source code in your `app.js` file. If you are following along with the LoanCalc sample app, this code should go after your ImageView logo which was added to the View from the previous recipe:

```
//create a label to identify the textfield to the user
var labelAmount = Titanium.UI.createLabel({
    width: 'auto',
    height: 30,
    top: 100,
    left: 20,
    font: {fontSize: 14, fontFamily: 'Helvetica',
        fontWeight:'bold'},},
    text: 'Loan amount:    $'
});
view.add(labelAmount);


//create a label to identify the textfield to the user
var labelInterestRate = Titanium.UI.createLabel({
    width: 'auto',
    height: 30,
    top: 150,
    left: 20,
    font: {fontSize: 14, fontFamily: 'Helvetica',
        fontWeight: 'bold'},
    text: 'Interest Rate:   %'
});
view.add(labelInterestRate);


//create a label to identify the textfield to the user
var labelLoanLength = Titanium.UI.createLabel({
    width: 100,
    height: 'auto',
    top: 200,
    left: 20,
    font: {fontSize: 14, fontFamily: 'Helvetica',
        fontWeight: 'bold'},
    text: 'Loan length (' + numberMonths + ' months):'
});

view.add(labelLoanLength);
```

How it works...

You should notice a trend by now in the way that Titanium instantiates objects and adds them to Views/Windows, as well as a trend in the way formatting is applied to most basic UI elements using the JavaScript object properties. Margins and padding are added using the absolute positioning values of `top` and `left`, while font styling is done with the standard CSS font properties; `fontSize`, `fontFamily` and `fontWeight` in the case of our example code.

A couple of important points to note:

▶ The `width` property of our first two labels is set to `auto`, which means Titanium will automatically calculate the width of the Label depending on the content inside (a string value in this case). This `auto` property can be used for both the width and height of many other UI elements as well (as you can see in the third label we created which has a dynamic height to match the Label's text). When no height or width properties are specified, the UI component will assume the exact dimensions of the parent view or window that encloses it.

▶ The `textAlign` property of the labels works the same way you'd expect it to in HTML. However, you will only notice the alignment of the text if the width of your label is not set to `auto` , unless that Label happens to spread over multiple lines.

Creating TextFields for user input

TextFields in Titanium are single-line textboxes used for capturing user input via the keyboard and usually form the most common UI element for user input in any application, along with Labels and Buttons. In this recipe we'll show you how to create a TextField, add it to your application's View, and use it to capture user input. We will style our TextField component by using a Constant value for the first time.

Getting ready

The complete source code for this recipe can be found in the /Chapter 1/Recipe 4 folder.

How to do it...

Type in the following code after the View is created but before we add that view to our Window. If you have been following along from the previous recipe, this code should be entered after your Labels were created:

```
//creating the textfield for our loan amount input
var tfAmount = Titanium.UI.createTextField({    width: 140,
  height: 30,
  top: 100,
  right: 20,
   borderStyle:Titanium.UI.INPUT_BORDERSTYLE_ROUNDED,
   returnKeyType:Titanium.UI.RETURNKEY_DONE,
  hintText: '1000.00'
});
view.add(tfAmount);

//creating the textfield for our percentage interest
//rate input
var tfInterestRate = Titanium.UI.createTextField({
  width: 140,
  height: 30,
  top: 150,
  right: 20,
   borderStyle:Titanium.UI.INPUT_BORDERSTYLE_ROUNDED,
   returnKeyType:Titanium.UI.RETURNKEY_DONE,
  value: interestRate
});

view.add(tfInterestRate);
```

How it works...

In this example, we are creating a couple of basic TextFields with a rounded border style and introducing some new property types that don't appear in Labels and ImageViews including `hintText`. The `hintText` property displays a value in the TextField that disappears when that TextField has focus (for example, when a user taps it to enter some data using their keyboard).

The user input is available in the TextField's property called `value`. As you will note in the previous recipe, accessing this value is simply a case of assigning it to a variable (that is `var myName = txtFirstName.value`), or alternatively using the value property directly.

There's more...

TextFields are one of the most common components in any application, and in Titanium, there are a couple of points and options to consider whenever using them.

Retrieving text...

It is important to note that when you want to retrieve the text a user has typed into a TextField, you need to reference the `value` property and not `text`, like many of the other string-based controls!

Experimenting with other TextField border styles...

Try experimenting with other TextField border styles to give your app a different appearance. Other possible values are:

```
Titanium.UI.INPUT_BORDERSTYLE_BEZEL
Titanium.UI.INPUT_BORDERSTYLE_LINE
Titanium.UI.INPUT_BORDERSTYLE_NONE
Titanium.UI.INPUT_BORDERSTYLE_ROUNDED
```

Working with keyboards and keyboard toolbars

When a TextField or TextArea control gains focus in either the iPhone or Android, the default keyboard is what springs up onto the screen. However, there will be times when you wish to change this behavior example, you may only want to have the user input numeric characters into a TextField when they are providing a numerical amount (such as their age, or a monetary value). Additionally, Keyboard Toolbars can be created to appear above the keyboard itself, which will allow you to provide the user with other options such as removing the keyboard from the Window, or allowing copy/paste operations via a simple button tap.

In the following recipe, we are going to create a toolbar that contains both a system button, and another system component called **FlexibleSpace**. These will be added to the top of our numeric keyboard which will appear whenever the TextField for amount or interest rate gains focus. Note that in this example we have updated the `tfAmount` and `tfInterestRate` TextField objects to now contain `keyboardType` and `returnKeyType` properties.

Getting ready

Note that toolbars are iPhone-specific, and that they may not be available for Android in the current Titanium SDK.

 The complete source code for this recipe can be found in the `/Chapter 1/Recipe 5` folder.

How to do it...

Open up your `app.js` file and type in the following code. If you have been following along from the previous recipe, this code should replace the previous recipe's code for adding the amount and interest rate TextFields:

```
//flexible space for button bars
var flexSpace = Titanium.UI.createButton({
  systemButton:Titanium.UI.iPhone.SystemButton.FLEXIBLE_SPACE
});

//done system button
var buttonDone = Titanium.UI.createButton({
    systemButton:Titanium.UI.iPhone.SystemButton.DONE,
    bottom: 0
});

//add the event listener 'click' event to our done button
buttonDone.addEventListener('click', function(e){
    tfAmount.blur();
    tfInterestRate.blur();
    tfInterestRate.top = 150;
    labelInterestRate.top = 150;
    interestRate = tfInterestRate.value;
    tfAmount.visible = true;
```

```
        labelAmount.visible = true;
    });

    //creating the textfield for our loan amount input
    var tfAmount = Titanium.UI.createTextField({
        width: 140,
        height: 30,
        top: 100,
        right: 20,
        borderStyle:Titanium.UI.INPUT_BORDERSTYLE_ROUNDED,
        returnKeyType:Titanium.UI.RETURNKEY_DONE,
        hintText: '1000.00',
        keyboardToolbar: [flexSpace,buttonDone],
        keyboardType:Titanium.UI.KEYBOARD_PHONE_PAD
    });
    view.add(tfAmount);
    //creating the textfield for our percentage interest rate //input
    var tfInterestRate = Titanium.UI.createTextField({
        width: 140,
        height: 30,
        top: 150,
        right: 20,
        borderStyle:Titanium.UI.INPUT_BORDERSTYLE_ROUNDED,
        returnKeyType:Titanium.UI.RETURNKEY_DONE,
        value: interestRate,
        keyboardToolbar: [flexSpace,buttonDone],
        keyboardType:Titanium.UI.KEYBOARD_PHONE_PAD
    });

    //if the interest rate is focused change its top value so we //can see
    it (only for the iphone platform though!)
    tfInterestRate.addEventListener('focus', function(e){
      if(Ti.Platform.osname == 'iphone') {
        tfInterestRate.top = 100;
        labelInterestRate.top = 100;
        tfAmount.visible = false;
        labelAmount.visible = false;
      }
    });

    view.add(tfInterestRate);
```

How it works...

In this recipe we are creating a TextField and adding it to our View. By now, you should have noticed how many properties are universal among the different UI components; `width`, `height`, `top`, and `right` are just four that are used in our TextField called `tfAmount` that have been used in previous recipes for other components. Many touch screen phones do not have physical keyboards; instead we are using a touch screen keyboard to gather our input data. Depending on the data you require, you may not need a full keyboard with all of the QWERTY keys and may want to just display a numeric keyboard (as seen in the following screenshot); such as when you were using the telephone dialling features on your iPhone or Android device. Additionally, you may require the QWERTY keys but in a specific format; custom keyboards make user input quicker and less frustrating for the user by presenting custom options such as keyboards for inputting web addresses and emails with all of the 'www' and '@' symbols in convenient touch locations.

There's more...

Try experimenting with other Keyboard styles in your Titanium app!

Experimenting with keyboard styles

Other possible values are:

```
Titanium.UI.KEYBOARD_DEFAULT
Titanium.UI.KEYBOARD_EMAIL
Titanium.UI.KEYBOARD_ASCII
Titanium.UI.KEYBOARD_URL
Titanium.UI.KEYBOARD_NUMBER_PAD
Titanium.UI.KEYBOARD_NUMBERS_PUNCTUATION
Titanium.UI.KEYBOARD_PHONE_PAD
```

Enhancing your App with Sliders & Switches

Sliders and Switches are two UI components that are simple to implement and can bring an extra level of interactivity to your apps. Switches, as the name suggests, have only two states—on and off—which are represented by Boolean values (*true* and *false*).

Sliders, on the other hand, take two float values, a minimum and maximum, and allow the user to select any number between and including these two values. In addition to it's default styling, the Slider API also allows you to use images for both sides of the 'track' and the 'slider thumb' image that runs along it. This allows you to create some truly customised designs.

We are going to add a Switch to indicate an on/off state and a Slider to hold the loan length, with values ranging from a minimum of 6 to a maximum of 72 months. Also, we'll add some event handlers to capture the changed value from each component, and in the case of the Slider, update an existing Label with the new Slider value. Don't worry if you aren't 100 percent sure about how event handlers work yet, as we will explain this in further detail in *Chapter 6, Getting To Grips With Events & Properties*.

Getting ready

The complete source code for this recipe can be found in the /Chapter 1/Recipe 6 folder.

How to do it...

If you are following with the LoanCalc app, the code below should be placed into your `window2.js` file for the Switch. We'll also add in a label to identify what the Switch component does and a View component to hold it all together:

```
//reference the current window var win1 = Titanium.UI.currentWindow;

//create the view, this will hold all of our UI controls
var view = Titanium.UI.createView({
  width: 300,
  height: 70,
  left: 10,
  top: 10,
  backgroundColor: '#fff',
  borderRadius: 5
});

//create a label to identify the switch control to the user
var labelSwitch = Titanium.UI.createLabel({
    width: 'auto',
    height: 30,
    top: 20,
    left: 20,
    font: {fontSize: 14, fontFamily: 'Helvetica',
           fontWeight: 'bold'},
    text: 'Auto Show Chart?'
});
view.add(labelSwitch);

//create the switch object
var switchChartOption = Titanium.UI.createSwitch({
  right: 20,
  top: 20,
  value: false
});
view.add(switchChartOption);


win1.add(view);
```

Now, let's write Slider code. Go back to your `app.js` file and type in the following code underneath the line `view.add(tfInterestRate);`:

```
//create the slider to change the loan length
var lengthSlider = Titanium.UI.createSlider({
  width: 140,
  top: 200,
  right: 20,
  min: 12,
  max: 60,
  value: numberMonths,
  thumbImage: 'sliderThumb.png',
  selectedThumbImage: 'sliderThumbSelected.png',
  highlightedThumbImage: 'sliderThumbSelected.png'
});

lengthSlider.addEventListener('change', function(e){
  //output the value to the console for debug
   Ti.API.info(lengthSlider.value);
   //update our numberMonths variable
  numberMonths = Math.round(lengthSlider.value);
   //update label
  labelLoanLength.text = 'Loan length (' + Math.round(numberMonths) +
' months):';
});
view.add(lengthSlider);
```

How it works...

In this recipe we are adding two new components to two separate Views within two separate Windows. The first component, a Switch, is fairly straight forward, and apart from the standard layout and positioning properties, takes one main Boolean value to determine its on or off status. It also has only the one event, `change`, which is executed whenever the Switch changes from the on to off position or vice versa.

On the Android platform, the Switch can be altered to appear as a toggle button (default) or as a checkbox. Additionally, Android users can also display a text label using the `title` property, which can be changed programmatically using the `titleOff` and `titleOn` properties.

The Slider component is more interesting and has many more properties than a Switch. Sliders are useful in instances where you want to allow the user to choose between a range of values, in our case, a numeric range of months from 12 to 60. For instance, this is a much more effective method of choosing a number from a range than it would be to list all of the possible options in a Picker, and a much safer way than letting a user enter in possibly invalid values via a TextField or TextArea component.

Pretty much all of the Slider can be styled using the default properties available in the Titanium API, including `thumbImage`, `selectedThumbImage`, and `highlightedThumbImage` as we have done in this recipe. The `highlightedThumbImage` works similar to how you might be used to in CSS. The image for the thumbnail in this case changes only when a user taps and holds on to the component in order to change its value.

There's more...

Try extending the styling of the Slider component by using images for the left and right hand sides of the 'track', which is the element that runs horizontally underneath the moving Switch itself.

Passing custom variables between windows

You will often find a need to pass variables and objects between different screen objects, such as Windows, in your apps. One example is between a master and child view. For example, if you have a tabular list of data that perhaps only shows a small amount of information per row and you wish to view the full description, you might pass that description data as a variable to the child window.

In this recipe, we are going to apply that same principle to a variable on the settings window (in the second tab of our LoanCalc app), by setting the variable in one window and then passing it back for use in our main window.

Getting ready

The complete source code for this recipe can be found in the /Chapter 1/Recipe 7 folder.

How to do it...

Under the declaration for your second window (win2) in your app.js file, add the following additional property called autoShowChart and set it to false. This is a custom property, that is, a property not already defined by the Titanium API. It is often handy to add additional properties to your objects if you require certain parameters that the API does not provide by default:

```
//
//////set the initial value of win2's custom property
win2.autoShowChart = false;
```

Now in the window2.js file that holds all of the sub components for your second window, add the following code extending the existing Switch control so it can update the referenced window's autoShowChart variable:

```
//create the switch object
var switchChartOption = Titanium.UI.createSwitch({
  right: 20,
  top: 20,
  value: false
});

//add the event listener for the switch when it changes
switchChartOption.addEventListener('change', function(e){
  win2.autoShowChart = switchChartOption.value;
```

```
});

//add the switch to the view
view.add(switchChartOption);
```

How it works...

This code is actually pretty straightforward. When an object is created in Titanium, all of the standard properties are accessible in a dictionary object of key-value pairs. All we are doing here is extending that dictionary object to add a property of our own.

We can do this in one of the two ways. First, as shown in our recipe's source code this can be done after the instantiation of the Window (`win2`) object. Second, it can also be done immediately within the instantiation code. In the source code of the second window, we are simply referencing this same object, so all of its properties are already available for us to read from and write to.

There's more...

There are other ways to pass and access objects and variables between Windows, including the use of App Properties. These will be covered in a later chapter.

Creating buttons and capturing click events

In any given app, you will find that creating buttons and capturing their click events is one of the most common tasks you will do. This recipe will show you how to declare a Button control in Titanium and attach the click event to it. Within that `click` event, we will perform a task and log it to the Info window in Titanium Studio.

This recipe will also demonstrate how to implement some of the default styling mechanisms available to you via the API.

Getting ready

The complete source code for this recipe can be found in the `/Chapter 1/Recipe 8` folder.

How to do it...

Open up your `app.js` file and type in the following code. If you're following along with the LoanCalc app, this code should go after you created and added the TextField controls to the View:

```
//calculate the interest for this loan button
var buttonCalculateInterest = Titanium.UI.createButton({
    image: 'calculateInterestButton.png',
   id: 1,
   top: 255,
   width: 252,
   height: 32,
   left: 23
});

//add the event listener
buttonCalculateInterest.addEventListener('click',
calculateAndDisplayValue);

//add the first button to our view
view.add(buttonCalculateInterest);

//calculate the interest for this loan button
var buttonCalculateRepayments = Titanium.UI.createButton({
    image: 'calculateRepaymentsButton.png',
   id: 2,
   top: 300,
   width: 252,
   height: 32,
   left: 23
});

//add the event listener
buttonCalculateRepayments.addEventListener('click',
                          calculateAndDisplayValue);

//add the second and final button to our view
view.add(buttonCalculateRepayments);
```

Now that we have created our two buttons and added their event listeners, let's extend the `calculateAndDisplayValue()` function to do some simple fixed interest mathematics and produce the results that we will log to the Titanium Studio console:

```
//add the event handler which will be executed when either of //our
calculation buttons are tapped
function calculateAndDisplayValue(e)
```

```
{
   //log the button id so we can debug which button was tapped
  Ti.API.info('Button id = ' + e.source.id);

   if (e.source.id == 1)
   {
      //Interest (I) = Principal (P) times Rate Per Period
      //(r) times Number of Periods (n) / 12
      var totalInterest = (tfAmount.value * (interestRate /
      100) * numberMonths) / 12;

      //log result to console
      Ti.API.info(totalInterest);
   }
   else
   {
      //Interest (I) = Principal (P) times Rate Per Period (r)
      //times Number of Periods (n) / 12
      var totalInterest = (tfAmount.value * (interestRate /
      100) * numberMonths) / 12;

      var totalRepayments = Math.round(tfAmount.value) +
      totalInterest;

      //log result to console
      Ti.API.info(totalRepayments);
   }

} //end function
```

How it works...

Most controls in Titanium are capable of firing one or more events, such as `focus`, `onload`, or as in our recipe, `click`. The `click` event is undoubtedly the one you will use more often than any other. In the previous source code, you'll note that in order to execute code from this event we are adding an event listener to our button, which has a signature of 'click'. This signature is a string and forms the first part of our event listener, the second part is the executing function for the event.

It's important to note that other component types can also be used in a similar manner. For example, an ImageView could be declared which contains a custom button image, and could have a click event attached to it in exactly the same way a regular button can.

Informing your users with dialogs and alerts

There are a number of dialogs available for you to use in the Titanium API, but for the purposes of this recipe we will be concentrating on the two main ones—the **AlertDialog** and the **OptionDialog**. These two simple components perform two similar roles, but with a key difference. The AlertDialog is normally only used to show the user a message, while the OptionDialog shows the user a message plus requires a response from them from a number of buttons. Generally, an AlertDialog only allows two standard responses from the user, OK or Cancel, whereas the OptionDialog can contain many more.

There are also key differences in the layout of these two dialog components which will become obvious in the recipe below.

Getting ready

The complete source code for this recipe can be found in the /Chapter 1/Recipe 9 folder.

How to do it...

First, we'll create an AlertDialog that simply notifies the user of an action that cannot be completed due to missing information—in our case, they have not provided a value for the loan amount in the tfAmount TextField:

```
if (tfAmount.value == '' || tfAmount.value == null)
{
    var errorDialog - Titanium.UI.createAlertDialog({
      title: 'Error!',
      message: 'You must provide a loan amount.'
    });
    errorDialog.show();
}
}
```

Now let's add the OptionDialog. The OptionDialog is going to display the result from our calculation and then give the user the choice to view the results as a Pie Chart (in a new window) or alternatively to cancel and remain on the same screen:

```
//check our win2 autoShowChart boolean value first (coming //from the
switch on window2.js)
if (win2.autoShowChart == true)
{
   openChartWindow();
}
else
{
   var resultOptionDialog = Titanium.UI.createOptionDialog({
                    title: optionsMessage + '\n\nDo you want to
            view this in a chart?',
                    options: ['Okay', 'No'],
                    cancel: 1
   });
```

```
            //add the click event listener to the option dialog
            resultOptionDialog.addEventListener('click', function(e){
                    Ti.API.info('Button index tapped was: ' + e.index);
                    if (e.index == 0)
                {
                        openChartWindow();
                }
            });

            resultOptionDialog.show();

    } //end if
```

How it works...

The AlertDialog is a very simple component that simply presents the user with a message as a modal and only has one possible response which closes the alert. Note that you should be careful not to call an AlertDialog more than once while a pending alert is still visible, for example, if you're calling that alert from within a loop.

The OptionDialog is a much larger modal component that presents a series of buttons with a message from the bottom of the screen and is generally used to allow the user to pick from a selection of more than one item. In our code, the `resultOptionDialog` presents the user with a choice of two options—"Okay" or "No". One interesting property on this dialog is **cancel**, which dismisses the dialog without firing the click event and also styles the button at the requested index in a manner that differentiates it from the rest of the group of buttons.

Just like the Window object, both of these dialogs are not added to another View but are presented by calling the `show()` method instead. You should only call the `show()` method after the dialog has been properly instantiated and any event listeners have been created.

The following screenshots show the difference between the AlertDialog and Option Dialog respectively:

There's more...

You can also create a predefined AlertDialog using basic JavaScript, using the syntax: `alert('Hello world!');`. Be aware though that you only have control over the contents of the message using this method, and the title of your AlertDialog will always be set to 'Alert'.

Creating charts using Raphael JS

Let's perform one final task for this application and for our first chapter; displaying charts and graphs. Titanium is without a native charting API, however, there are some open source options for implementing charts such as Google Charts. While the Google solution is free, it requires your apps to be online every time you need to generate a chart. This might be okay for some circumstances, but it's not the best solution for any application that is meant to be used offline. Plus, Google Charts returns a generated JPG or PNG file at the requested size and in a rasterized format which is not great for zooming in when viewed on an iPhone or iPad.

A better solution is to use the open source and MIT licensed Raphael library which, luckily for us, has a charting component! Not only is it free, but Raphael is also completely vector based, meaning any charts you create will look great on any resolution, and can be zoomed in without a loss of quality.

 Note that this recipe may not work on all Android devices as the current version of Raphael is not supported by non-webkit mobile browsers. However, it will work as described here for the iPhone and iPod Touch.

Getting ready

1. Download the main Raphael JS library from `http://raphaeljs.com` (Direct link: `http://github.com/DmitryBaranovskiy/raphael/raw/master/raphael-min.js`).

2. Download the main Charting library from `http://g.raphaeljs.com` (Direct link: `http://github.com/DmitryBaranovskiy/g.raphael/blob/master/g.raphael-min.js?raw=true`) and any other charting libraries you wish to use.

For this example, we are implementing the Pie Chart, which is here: `http://github.com/DmitryBaranovskiy/g.raphael/blob/master/g.pie-min.js?raw=true`.

 The complete source code for this recipe can be found in the `/Chapter 1/Recipe 10` folder.

How to do it...

1. Create a new project in Titanium Studio (or alternatively, if you're following along with the LoanCalc example app, then open your project directory), and put your downloaded files into a new folder called **charts** under your **Resources** directory. You could put them into the root folder if you wish, but bear in mind, you'd need to ensure your references in the following steps are correct.

2. The next step is to rename your `raphael-min.js` file to `raphael-min.lib`. The main reason is that if your file is a known JavaScript file (as in it ends in '`.js`'), the JSLint validator in Titanium will try to validate the Raphael JS library and fail, causing Titanium to lock up. This means you won't be able to run your app and will need to restart Titanium Studio!

3. Create a WebView in your app, referencing a variable holding the HTML code to display a Raphael chart, which we will call **chartHTML**. A WebView is a UI component that allows you to display web pages or HTML in your application. It does not include any features of a fully-fledged browser such as navigation controls or an address bar. Type in the following code at the top of your `chartwin.js` file, just after you have included the charting library and created titles for the chart view:

```
var chartWin = Titanium.UI.currentWindow;

//include the chart library
Titanium.include('charts/chart.js');

//create the chart title using the variables we passed in from
//app.js (our first window)
var chartTitleInterest = 'Total Interest: $' +
                         chartWin.totalInterest;
var chartTitleRepayments = 'Total Repayments: $' +
                           chartWin.totalRepayments;

//create the chart using the sample html from the
//raphaeljs.com website
var chartHTML = '<html><head> <title>RaphaelJS Chart</
title><meta name="viewport" content="width=device-width, initial-
scale=1.0"/>        <script src="charts/raphael.js.lib" type="text/
javascript" charset="utf-8"></script>    <script src="charts/g.
raphael-min.lib" type="text/javascript" charset="utf-8"></
script>    <script src="charts/g.pie-min.lib" type="text/
javascript" charset="utf-8"></script>    <script type="text/
javascript" charset="utf-8">            window.onload = function
() {              var r = Raphael("chartDiv");  r.g.txtattr.font
= "12px Verdana, Tahoma, sans-serif";  r.g.text(150, 10, "';

chartHTML = chartHTML + chartTitleInterest + '").attr({"font-
size": 14}); r.g.text(150, 30, "' + chartTitleRepayments + '").
attr({"font-size": 14});';

chartHTML = chartHTML + ' r.g.piechart(150, 180, 130, [' + Math.
round(chartWin.totalInterest) + ',' + Math.round(chartWin.
principalRepayments) + ']); };    </script> </head><body>    <div
id="chartDiv" style="width:320px; height: 320px; margin: 0"></div>
</body></html>';

//add a webview to contain our chart
```

```
var webview = Titanium.UI.createWebView({
    width: 320,
    height: 367,
    top: 0,
    html: chartHTML
});
chartWin.add(webview);
```

4. Now back in your `app.js` file, create a new function called `openChartWindow()`
    which will be executed when the user chooses "Okay" from the previous recipe's
    option dialog. This function will create a new Window object based on the
    `chartwin.js` file and pass to it the values needed to show the chart:

```
//we'll call this function if the user opts to view the loan //
chart
function openChartWindow(totalInterest, total)
{
    //Interest (I) = Principal (P) times Rate Per Period (r)
    //times Number of Periods (n) / 12
    var totalInterest = (tfAmount.value * (interestRate / 100)
                        * numberMonths) / 12;
    var totalRepayments = Math.round(tfAmount.value) +
                        totalInterest;

    var chartWindow = Titanium.UI.createWindow({
        url: 'chartwin.js',
        title: 'Loan Pie Chart',
        barImage: 'navbar.png',
        barColor: '#000',
        numberMonths: numberMonths,
        interestRate: interestRate,
        totalInterest: totalInterest,
        totalRepayments: totalRepayments,
        principalRepayments: (totalRepayments - totalInterest)
    });

    tab1.open(chartWindow);
}
```

How it works...

Essentially what we are doing here is wrapping the Raphael library, something that originally
was built for the desktop browser, into a format that can be consumed and displayed using
the iPhone's WebKit browser. Raphael was originally created to simplify vector graphics
generation on the web and was extended later on as gRaphael in order to render both static
and interactive charts.

There is a series of documentation on Raphael at `http://raphaeljs.com` and `http://g.raphaeljs.com` on how it renders charts via its JavaScript library. We will not be explaining this in detail but rather the implementation of the library to work with Titanium.

Our implementation consists firstly of including the `charts.js` library from Raphael into our Titanium project. This is the main source file used by the library. From there, we are creating a new type of component, a WebView, which will (in this case) hold the HTML data that we constructed in the variable `chartHTML`. This HTML data contains all of the includes necessary to render the charts, which are listed in item #2 of the *Getting Ready* section of this recipe. If you had a chart with static data, you could also reference the HTML from a file using the `url` property of the WebView object instead of passing in all of the HTML as a string. The chart itself is created using some simple JavaScript embedded in HTML data string, r.g.piechart(150, 180, 130, n1, n2), where n1 and n2 are the two values we wish to display as slices in the Pie Chart. The other values define the center point of the chart from the top and left respectively, followed by the chart radius.

All of this is wrapped up in a new Window defined by the `chartwin.js` file, which accesses properties passed in from the first tab's Window in our LoanCalc app. This data is passed using exactly the same mechanism as explained in the previous "*Passing Custom Variables Between Windows*" recipe.

The following screenshot shows the Raphael JS Library being used to show a pie chart based on our loan data:

2
Working with Local and Remote Data Sources

In this chapter, we will cover:

- ▶ Reading data from remote XML through HTTPClient
- ▶ Displaying data using a TableView
- ▶ Enhancing your TableView with custom rows
- ▶ Filtering your TableView with the SearchBar control
- ▶ Speeding up your remote data access using JSON and Yahoo! YQL
- ▶ Creating an SQLite database
- ▶ Saving data locally using an SQLite database
- ▶ Retrieving data from an SQLite database
- ▶ Creating a "pull and release" refresh mechanism

Introduction

Fully understanding the methods available to you in Titanium Studio when it comes to reading, parsing, and saving data, is fundamental to the success of the apps you will build. Titanium provides you with all of the tools that you will need to make everything from simple XML calls over HTTP, implementing JSON for improved network speeds, to complex applications running a localized relational database (SQLite) for offline storage requirements.

In this chapter we will not only cover the fundamental methods of implementing remote data access over HTTP, but also how to store and present that data effectively using TableViews, TableRows, and other customized user interfaces.

Pre-requisites

You should have a basic understanding of both the XML and JSON data formats, which are widely-used standardized methods of transporting data across the Web. Additionally, you should also understand what **SQL** (**Structured Query Language**) is and how to create basic SQL statements such as CREATE, SELECT, DELETE, and INSERT. There is a great beginners introduction to SQL at `http://sqlzoo.net` if you need to refer to tutorials on how to perform common types of database queries.

Reading data from remote XML through HTTPClient

The ability to consume and display feed data from the Internet, through RSS feeds or alternate APIs, is the cornerstone of many mobile applications. More importantly, many services that you may wish to integrate into your app will probably require you to do this at some point or another, such as Twitter or Wikipedia, so it is vital to understand and be able to implement remote data feeds and XML. Our first recipe for this chapter introduces some new functionality within Titanium to help address this need.

If you are intending to follow the entire chapter and build the MyRecipes app, then pay careful attention to the first *Getting Ready* section for this recipe, as it will guide you through setting up the project.

Getting ready

To prepare for this recipe, open up Titanium Studio and log in if you have not already done so. If you need to register a new account, you can do so for free directly from within the application. Once you are logged in, click on **New Project**, and the details window for creating a new project will appear. Enter **MyRecipes** as the name of the app, and fill in the rest of the details with your own information.

 Pay attention to the app identifier, which is written normally in reverse domain notation (that is *com.packtpub.myrecipes*). This identifier cannot be easily changed after the project is created and you will need to match it *exactly* when creating provisioning profiles for distributing your apps later on.

Complete source code for this entire chapter can be found in the /Chapter 2/ RecipeFinder folder, while source code for this recipe can be found in the /Chapter 2/ Recipe 1 folder.

How to do it...

Now our project shell is set up, so let's get down to business! First, open your app.js file, and two more JavaScript files called recipes.js and favorites.js. In your app.js, reference recipes.js and favorites.js to win1 and win2 respectively, and give each window a meaningful title (for example, "Recipes"). We'll also change the tab icons from their defaults to the two icons 'fork-and-knife.png' and 'heart.png' respectively. Both of these icons are available in the accompanying source files.

Open the recipes.js file in your IDE. This is the file that will hold our code for retrieving and displaying recipes from a RSS feed. Type in the following code at the top of your recipes.js file. This code will create an HTTPClient and read in the feed XML from the recipes website.

```
var win = Titanium.UI.currentWindow;

//declare the http client object
var xhr = Titanium.Network.createHTTPClient();

//this method will process the remote data
xhr.onload = function() {
  Ti.API.info(this.responseText);
};

//this method will fire if there's an error in accessing the //remote
data
xhr.onerror = function() {
  //log the error to our Titanium Studio console
  Ti.API.error(this.status + ' - ' + this.statusText);
};

//open up the recipes xml feed
xhr.open('GET', 'http://www.cuisine.com.au/feed/all-recipes');

//finally, execute the call to the remote feed
xhr.send();
```

Try running the emulator now for either Android or iPhone. You should have two tabs appear on the screen as shown next, and, after a few seconds, a stack of XML data printed out to your Titanium Studio console log.

```
[INFO] Application started
[INFO] RecipeFinder/1.0 (1.8.0.8169a91)
[INFO] <?xml version="1.0"?>
<rss version="2.0">
<channel>
<title>Cuisine - All Cuisine recipes</title>
<link>http://cuisine.com.au/recipe-finder/all-recipes</link>
<description>Hundreds of delicious and free cooking recipes.</description>
<language>en-au</language>
<item>
<title>Sugared berries with passionfruit curd</title>
<link>http://cuisine.com.au/recipe/Sugared-berries-with-passionfruit-curd</link>
<description></description>
</item>
<item>
<title>Nasi Goreng</title>
<link>http://cuisine.com.au/recipe/Nasi-Goreng-kate-gibbs</link>
<description>A good nasi goreng, meaning "fried rice", is no ordinary staple food but a complete meal of
flavours, spices, garnishes and accompaniments. In Indonesian households, the previous night's leftovers often
prescribe the ingredients for the dish, with crunchy, fresh elements added on the day. Shredded cooked chicken
breast, green beans, cooked prawns or fish can be tossed into the fried rice at the end of cooking if they are on
hand.
In Jakarta, a hefty dose of garlic and fried shrimp are usually added, as well as a few sticks of satay to dip in
peanut sauce.
Cook the egg yolk so it's still a little runny, to give the fried rice a sticky sauce when pierced at the table.
This is one of the most interesting, quickest and easiest things you can make with leftover cooked
rice.</description>
</item>
```

How it works...

If you are already familiar with JavaScript for the web, this should make a lot of sense to you. Here we are creating an `HTTPClient` using the `Titanium.Network` namespace, and opening a `GET` connection on the URL of the feed from the recipes website, using an object called `xhr`.

By implementing the `onload` event listener, we can capture the XML data that has been retrieved by the `xhr` object. In the source code you will note that we have used `Ti.API.info()` to echo information to the Titanium Studio screen, which is a great way to debug and follow events in your app. If your connection and `GET` request was successful, you should see a large XML string outputted in the Titanium Studio info log. The final piece of the recipe is small but very important—calling the `xhr` object's `send()` method. This kicks off the `GET` request. Without it, your app would never load any data. It is important to note that you will not receive any errors or warnings if you forget to implement `xhr.send()`. If your app is not receiving any data, this is the first place to check.

If you are having trouble parsing your XML, always check if it is valid first! Opening up the XML feed in your browser will normally provide you with enough information to determine whether your feed is valid, or if it has broken elements.

Displaying data using a TableView

TableViews are the most used components in the entire iPhone and Android SDKs, almost all of the native apps on your device will utilize tables in some shape or form. They are used to display large lists of data in an effective manner, allowing for scrolling lists that can be customized visually, searched upon, or drilled to expose child views. With so many available properties and options, it's easy to get lost in the functionality and ability of these components. Luckily for us, Titanium makes it easy to implement TableViews into your application. In this recipe, we will implement a TableView and use our XML data feed from the previous recipe to populate it with a list of recipes.

 Complete source code for this recipe can be found in the /Chapter 2/Recipe 2 folder.

How to do it...

Once we have connected our app to a data feed and we're retrieving XML data via the XHR object, we need to be able to manipulate that data and display it into a TableView component. Firstly, create an array object called `data` at the top of your `recipes.js` file. This array will hold all of the information for our TableView in a global context:

```
var data = []; //empty data array
```

We are now going to disseminate the XML and read in the required elements to our `data` array object, before finally creating a TableView and assigning its `data` property to our `data` object:

```
//declare the http client object
var xhr = Titanium.Network.createHTTPClient();

//create the table view
var tblRecipes = Titanium.UI.createTableView({
```

```
    height: 366,
    width: 320,
    top: 0,
    left: 0
});
win.add(tblRecipes);

//this method will process the remote data
xhr.onload = function() {

  var xml = this.responseXML;
  //get the item nodelist from our response xml object
  var items = xml.documentElement.getElementsByTagName("item");

  //loop each item in the xml
  for (var i = 0; i < items.length; i++) {

    //create a table row
    var row = Titanium.UI.createTableViewRow({
      title:
      items.item(i).getElementsByTagName("title").item(0).text
    });

    //add the table row to our data[] object
    data.push(row);

  } //end for loop

//finally, set the data property of the tableView to our //data[]
object
tblRecipes.data = data;

};
```

The following screenshot shows the Table view with the titles of our recipes from the XML feed:

How it works...

The first thing you will notice is that we are using the `Ti.XML` namespace to assign the list of elements to a new object called `items`. This allows us to use a `for` loop construct in order to loop through the items and assign each individual item to the `data` array object we created and gave a global scope.

From there we are creating our TableView by implementing the `Titanium.UI.createTableView()` function. You should notice almost immediately that many of our regular properties are also used by tables, including width, height, and positioning. However, a TableView has one extra and important property—data. The data property accepts an array of data, the values of which can either be used dynamically (as we have done here with the title property) or can be assigned to sub-component children of a TableRow. As you begin to build more complex applications you will learn to fully understand just how flexible table-based layouts can be.

Enhancing your TableViews with custom rows

So far we have created a TableView, which while being totally usable and showing the names of our recipes from the XML feed, is a bit bland. To customize our table we will need to create and add custom TableRow objects to an array of rows, which we can then assign to our TableView object. Each of these TableRow objects is essentially a type of View, to which we can add any number of components, such as Labels, ImageViews, and Buttons.

Next, we will create our TableRow objects and add to each one of them the name of the recipe from our XML feed, a short description, and a thumbnail image (which we will get from the `images` folder in our `Resources` directory) to each one of them. If you do not already have an images directory, create one now and copy the images from the source code for this recipe, which can be found in the `/Chapter 2/Recipe 3` folder.

How to do it...

Open your `recipe.js` file and type in the following code. If you have been following along with the previous recipe, then the following code will extend what you have already written:

```
var data = []; //empty data array

//declare the http client object
var xhr = Titanium.Network.createHTTPClient();

var tblRecipes = Titanium.UI.createTableView({
  height: 366,
  width: 320,
  top: 0,
  left: 0,
  rowHeight: 70
});
win.add(tblRecipes);

//this method will process the remote data
xhr.onload = function() {
  var xml = this.responseXML;

  //get the item nodelist from our response xml object
  var items = xml.documentElement.getElementsByTagName("item");

  //loop each item in the xml
  for (var i = 0; i < items.length; i++) {
```

```
//create a table row
var row = Titanium.UI.createTableViewRow({
  hasChild: true,
  className: 'recipe-row'
});

//title label
var titleLabel = Titanium.UI.createLabel({
  text:
  items.item(i).getElementsByTagName("title").item(0).text,
  font: {fontSize: 14, fontWeight: 'bold'},
  left: 70,
  top: 5,
  height: 20,
  width: 210
});
row.add(titleLabel);

//description label
var descriptionLabel = Titanium.UI.createLabel({
  text:
  items.item(i).getElementsByTagName("description").item(0).text,
  font: {fontSize: 10, fontWeight: 'normal'},
  left: 70,
  top: 25,
  height: 40,
  width: 200
});
if(descriptionLabel.text == '') {
  descriptionLabel.text = 'No description is available.';
}
row.add(descriptionLabel);

//add our little icon to the left of the row
var iconImage = Titanium.UI.createImageView({
  image: 'images/foodicon.jpg',
  width: 50,
  height: 50,
  left: 10,
  top: 10
});
row.add(iconImage);
//add the table row to our data[] object
data.push(row);
}
```

```
    //finally, set the data property of the tableView to our
    //data[] object
    tblRecipes.data = data;

};
```

How it works...

One thing that should be immediately obvious is that a **TableRow** object can contain any number of components which you can define and add in the standard way (see *Chapter 1, Building Apps Using Native UI Components*, for examples of implementing different UI components).

What is the `className` property used for then? When rows are rendered on your device it all happens on request, that is, only those rows which are visible are actually rendered by the OS, which can be seen in the following screenshots. The reasons for this are two-fold. First, to conserve memory, of which most devices have precious little in comparison to desktop computers. Second, to help speed up your application by only performing those CPU tasks which are absolutely necessary.

For a few rows, the memory usage without using a `className` will not be too high, but for many rows, depending on how many and what interface components you are using within the row, your app will load very slowly or may even crash.

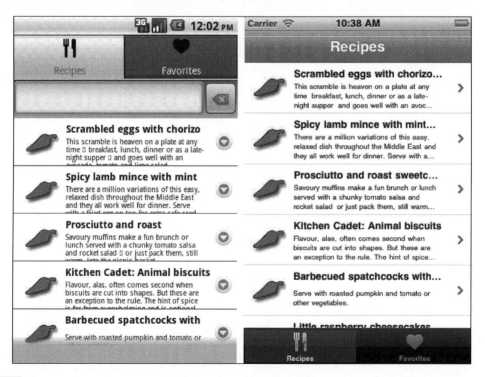

Filtering the TableView using a SearchBar component

So what happens when your user wants to search all data in your TableView? By far the easiest way is to use the **SearchBar** component. This is a standard control that consists of a searchable text field with an optional cancel button, and attaches to the top of your table view using the table view's `searchBar` property.

In this next recipe, we will implement a search bar into our **MyRecipes** app that filters our recipes based on the `title` property.

 Complete source code for this recipe can be found in the `/Chapter 2/Recipe 4` folder.

How to do it...

First of all, create a `searchBar` component before your `tableView` is defined, and then create the event listener's for the `searchBar`.

```
//define our search bar which will attach
//to our table view
var searchBar = Titanium.UI.createSearchBar({
  showCancel:true,
  height:43,
  top:0
});

//print out the searchbar value whenever it changes
searchBar.addEventListener('change', function(e){
  //search the tableview as user types
  Ti.API.info('user searching for: ' + e.value);
});

//when the return key is hit, remove focus from
//our searchBar
searchBar.addEventListener('return', function(e){
  searchBar.blur();
});

//when the cancel button is tapped, remove focus
//from our searchBar
searchBar.addEventListener('cancel', function(e){
  searchBar.blur();
});
```

Now set the search property of our tableView to our searchBar component, and then set the `filterAttribute` of our tableView to `'filter'`. We will define this custom property called `'filter'` within each of our row objects.

```
//define our table view
var tblRecipes = Titanium.UI.createTableView({
  height: 366,
  width: 320,
  top: 0,
  left: 0,
  rowHeight: 70,
  search: searchBar,
  filterAttribute:'filter' //here is the search filter which
                           //appears in TableViewRow
});


win.add(tblRecipes);
```

Now, inside each row that you define when looping through our xml data, add a custom property called `'filter'` and set it's value to the title text from the XML feed:

```
//this method will process the remote data
xhr.onload = function() {
  var xml = this.responseXML;

  //get the item nodelist from our response xml object
  var items = xml.documentElement.getElementsByTagName("item");

  //loop each item in the xml
  for (var i = 0; i < items.length; i++) {

    //create a table row
    var row = Titanium.UI.createTableViewRow({
      hasChild: true,
      className: 'recipe-row',
      filter: items.item(i).getElementsByTagName("title").item(0).text
//this is the data we want to search on (title)
    });
```

That's it! Run your project and you should now have a search bar attached to your table view as shown in the following screenshot. Tap it and type in any part of a recipe's title to see the results filtered in your table.

How it works...

In the first block of code, we are simply defining our **SearchBar** object like any other UI component, before attaching it to the `searchBar` property of our TableView in the second block of code. The event listeners for the `searchBar` simply ensure that when the user taps either one of the '**Search**' or '**Cancel**' buttons, the focus on the text input is lost and the keyboard will therefore become hidden.

The final block of code defines just what data we are searching for, in this case, our `filter` property has been set to the title of the recipes. This property needs to be added to each row that we define before it is bound to our TableView.

Speeding up your remote data access using JSON and Yahoo! YQL

If you are already familiar with using JavaScript heavily for the web, particularly when using popular libraries such as jQuery or Prototype, then you may already be aware of the benefits of using JSON instead of XML. The JSON data format is much less verbose than XML, meaning the file size is smaller and data transfer much faster. This is particularly important when a user on a mobile device may be limited in data speed due to network access and bandwidth.

If you have never seen Yahoo's YQL console, or heard of the YQL language web service, it is essentially a free web service that allows developers and applications to query, filter, and combine separate data sources from across the Internet.

In this recipe, we are going to use the Yahoo! YQL console and web service to obtain data from our recipes data feed and transform that data into a JSON object, which we will then bind to our TableView.

 Complete source code for this recipe can be found in the /Chapter 2/Recipe 5 folder.

How to do it...

First of all, go to Yahoo's YQL console page by opening up `http://developer.yahoo.com/yql/console` in your browser. On the right-hand side of the browser window you should notice a section called '**Data Tables**'. Select '**data**' and then '**feed**' from the data tables list. Your SQL statement should automatically change to a simple data feed from the Yahoo! News Network. Now, replace the URL value in the YQL statement to our recipe's feed, which is `http://www.cuisine.com.au/feed/all-recipes`, select '**JSON**' instead of **XML** from the radio buttons below, and click on '**Test**' as shown in the following screenshot. You should see a formatted set of data return in the results window in JSON format!

To use this data we need to copy and paste the full REST query from the YQL console. This is right at the bottom of the browser and is a single-line textbox. Copy and paste the entire URL into your `xhr.open()` method, replacing the existing recipes feed URL.

Make sure when you paste the string in, it hasn't broken due to any apostrophes. If it has, you will need to escape any apostrophe characters by replacing **'** with **\'**. You may also want to remove the `&callback=cbfunc` parameter from the URL as it can sometimes cause the JSON to stop parsing.

Now, back in the `xhr.onload()` function, let's replace all of the XML parsing code with code to parse our data in JSON format instead:

```
//this method will process the remote data
xhr.onload = function() {
  //create a json object using the JSON.PARSE function
  var jsonObject = JSON.parse(this.responseText);

  //print out how many items we have to the console
  Ti.API.info(jsonObject.query.results.item.length);
```

```
//loop each item in the json object
for(var i = 0; i < jsonObject.query.results.item.length; i++) {
  //create a table row
  var row = Titanium.UI.createTableViewRow({
    hasChild: true,
    className: 'recipe-row',
    backgroundColor: '#fff',
    filter: jsonObject.query.results.item[i].title
            //this is the data we want to search on (title)
  });

  //title label
  var titleLabel = Titanium.UI.createLabel({
    text: jsonObject.query.results.item[i].title,
    font: {fontSize: 14, fontWeight: 'bold'},
    left: 70,
    top: 5,
    height: 20,
    width: 210,
    color: '#000'
  });
  row.add(titleLabel);

  //description label
  var descriptionLabel = Titanium.UI.createLabel({
    text: jsonObject.query.results.item[i].description,
    font: {fontSize: 10, fontWeight: 'normal'},
    left: 70,
    top: 25,
    height: 40,
    width: 200,
    color: '#000'
  });
  if(descriptionLabel.text == '') {
    descriptionLabel.text = 'No description is
                            available.';
  }
  row.add(descriptionLabel);

  //add our little icon to the left of the row
  var iconImage = Titanium.UI.createImageView({
    image: 'images/foodicon.jpg',
    width: 50,
    height: 50,
```

```
      left: 10,
      top: 10
    });
    row.add(iconImage);

    //add the table row to our data[] object
    data.push(row);
  }

  //finally, set the data property of the tableView
  //to our data[] object
  tblRecipes.data = data;
};

//this method will fire if there's an error in accessing
//the remote data
xhr.onerror = function() {
  //log the error to our Titanium Studio console
  Ti.API.error(this.status + ' - ' + this.statusText);
};

//open up the recipes xml feed
xhr.open('GET', 'http://query.yahooapis.com/v1/public/yql?q=select%20
*%20from%20feed%20where%20url%3D%22http%3A%2F%2Fwww.cuisine.com.
au%2Ffeed%2Fall-recipes%22&format=json&diagnostics=false');

//finally, execute the call to the remote feed
xhr.send();
```

How it works...

As you can see in this recipe, accessing the YQL web service is simply a matter of passing an HTTP GET query to the YQL service URL, using a YQL statement as a URL parameter. When it processes a query, the Yahoo! YQL service obtains and transforms the requested data and returns in your specified format (in our case, JSON).

Accessing the properties of the JSON data object is also different, and arguably much simpler, as compared to XML. In JSON we use simple dot notation to navigate the data tree hierarchy and select the property we want to use. If you already understand the array syntax in PHP, Javascript, and a number of other C-Style languages, this should be pretty familiar to you!

There's more...

Throughout this chapter we have only been using a single RSS feed source, but what if you have multiple RSS feeds that you wish to read in simultaneously?

Combining multiple RSS feeds...

The answer to the previous question is to use Yahoo! Pipes—a free service provided by Yahoo! that let's you create a "pipe" consisting of one or more RSS, JSON, or data feeds which can be filtered and sorted before allowing you to output the data to a single feed. Give it a try by signing up for free at `http://pipes.yahoo.com`.

Creating an SQLite database

There are many reasons why SQLite has become the relational database of choice for mobile handsets—it is scalable, fast, written in native C, and very portable, and has the added bonus of an exceptionally small footprint. We need local databases on our devices in order to store data when devices are offline, or even to store data that is only required locally (high scores in a game, for instance).

Additionally, the caching of remote data can help speed up data access times in our applications—particularly important when mobile devices may have limited connectivity and bandwidth.

There are two ways to create SQLite databases in your application, one—create the database in code using SQL and two—copy and attach an existing database to your app via the 'install' method. In this recipe we will explain how to create a database via SQL statements.

 Complete source code for this recipe can be found in the `/Chapter 1/Recipe 6` folder.

How to do it...

Create a new JavaScript file called `database.js`, and type in the following code at the top of your new file:

```
//create the database object
var db = Titanium.Database.open('mydb');
db.execute('CREATE TABLE IF NOT EXISTS favorites (ID INTEGER  PRIMARY
KEY AUTOINCREMENT, TITLE TEXT, LINK TEXT, DESCRIPTION TEXT)');
```

Now add the following line to the top of each Window that we need to reference our database functions from. Do this to both your `recipes.js` and `favorites.js` files.

```
Ti.include('database.js');
```

How it works...

One of the great things about SQLite is the simplicity of its creation. In the previous example code, you can see we are not even performing a "create database" query anywhere. Simply attempting to open a database that does not exist, in this case `mydb`, tells the SQLite engine to create it automatically!

From there we can create our SQL table using standard SQL syntax. In our case, we have created a table with an ID that is both the primary key and an auto-incrementing number, a title, link, and description. The latter three fields match the data being returned from our recipes data source. In the next recipe we can use this table to locally store our recipe data.

There's more...

Let's take a look at attaching a pre-populated database file.

Attaching a pre-populated database file...

Should you wish to create your database separately and attach it to your application at runtime, there is a method called `Titanium.Database.install()`. Implementing this method is very easy, as it just accepts two parameters—the database file and the database name. As an example:

```
Var db = Titanium.Database.install('data.db', 'packtData');
```

There are also numerous free SQLite applications for creating and managing SQLite databases. The open source **SQLite Database Browser** tool is freely available from `http://sqlitebrowser.sourceforge.net` and runs on Windows, Linux, and Mac OS X.

Saving data locally using an SQLite database

Saving and updating data to your SQLite database is just a matter of creating a function for each CRUD operation you need, and forming the SQL statement before executing it against the local database (our 'db' object).

In this recipe, we will edit the `database.js` file to contain two new functions, one for inserting a record in our favorites table and one for deleting a record. We will also capture the click events on our Table Rows to allow the user to view the record in a detailed sub-window, and add a button for creating the favorite.

Complete source code for this recipe can be found in the /Chapter 2/Recipe 7 folder.

How to do it...

Open your JavaScript file called database.js, and type in the following code at the top of your new file, after your table creation script:

```
function insertFavorite(title, description, link) {
  var sql = "INSERT INTO favorites (title, description, link) VALUES
(";
  sql = sql + "'" + title.replace("'", "''") + "', ";
  sql = sql + "'" + description.replace("'", "''") + "', ";
  sql = sql + "'" + link.replace("'", "''") + "')";
  db.execute(sql);
  return db.lastInsertRowId;
}

function deleteFavorite(id) {
  var sql = "DELETE FROM favorites WHERE id = " + id;
  db.execute(sql);
}
```

Then, back in our recipes.js file, we are going to capture the click event of the tblRecipes TableView in order to get the tapped row's data and save it to our favorites table in SQLite:

```
//create a new window and pass through data from the
//tapped row
tblRecipes.addEventListener('click', function(e){
  var selectedRow = e.rowData; //row index clicked
  var detailWindow = Titanium.UI.createWindow({
    title: selectedRow._title,
    _description: selectedRow._description,
    _link: selectedRow._link,
    backgroundColor: '#fff',
    id: 0
  });

  //add the favorite button
  var favButton = Titanium.UI.createButton({
    title: 'Add Favorite',
    left: 10,
    top: 10,
```

```
    width: 140,
    height: 30,
    added: 0
});
favButton.addEventListener('click',function(e){
  if (favButton.added == 0) {
    var newId = insertFavorite(detailWindow.title,
      detailWindow._description, detailWindow._link);
    Ti.API.info('Newly created favorite id = ' + newId);
    detailWindow.id = newId;
    alert('This recipe has been added as a favorite!');
    favButton.added = 1;
    favButton.title = 'Remove Favorite';
  }
  else {
    deleteFavorite(detailWindow.id);
    Ti.API.info('Deleted ' + affectedRows +
      ' favorite records. (id ' + detailWindow.id + ')');
    detailWindow.id = 0;
    alert('This recipe has been removed from favorites!');
    favButton.added = 0;
    favButton.title = 'Add Favorite';
  }
});

 detailWindow.add(favButton);

//let's also add a button to open a link in safari
var linkButton = Titanium.UI.createButton({
  title: 'View In Safari',
  right: 10,
  top: 10,
  width: 140,
  height: 30,
  added: 0
});

//this event listener will open the link in safari
linkButton.addEventListener('click',function(e){
  Ti.Platform.openURL(detailWindow._link);
});

detailWindow.add(linkButton);
```

```
//finally, add the full description so we can read the
//whole recipe
var lblDescription = Titanium.UI.createLabel({
  text: detailWindow._description,
  left: 10,
  top: 50,
  width: 300,
  height: 'auto',
  color: '#000'
});

  detailWindow.add(lblDescription);

//open the detail window
  Titanium.UI.currentTab.open(detailWindow);
});
```

How it works...

First, we are creating functions that will accept the parameters to insert a favorite record, creating an SQL statement, and then executing that SQL query statement against our SQLite database. This is just a basic SQL query, although take note that just as you would with a desktop application or website, any input parameters should be escaped properly to avoid SQL injection! We're using a simple mechanism to do this in our recipe by simply replacing any occurrences of the apostrophe characters with a double apostrophe.

The second half of our code defines a new Window and adds to it a couple of buttons and a label for displaying the full text of our recipe. You should refer to *Chapter 1, Building Apps Using Native UI Components,* for more details on opening Windows, and adding and customizing UI components to them. One final point of interest, and a method we haven't come across before, is `Ti.Platform.openURL()`. This method simply takes a valid URL and launches the Safari browser (or Android browser) on your phone. In our recipe, we're passing the "link" property from our data so the user can view the recipe in full from it's original website.

There's more...

Android users can always press their back button on the device to return to the app after the browser is launched, but it's worth noting that iPhone users would need to close Safari and re-launch the application from their home screen after the link button has been pressed. To avoid this, you could create another sub-window containing a WebView component, opening this through the `Titanium.UI.currentTab.open()` method, just as we did for our detail view in this recipe.

The following screenshots show the detail view window for our recipe, before and after we insert a favorite record into the SQLite database table.

For an iPhone:

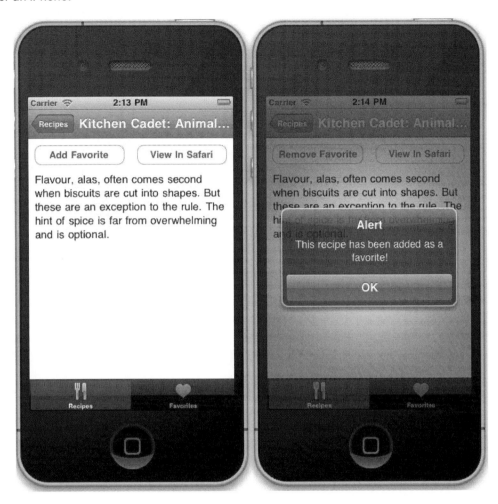

For an Android phone:

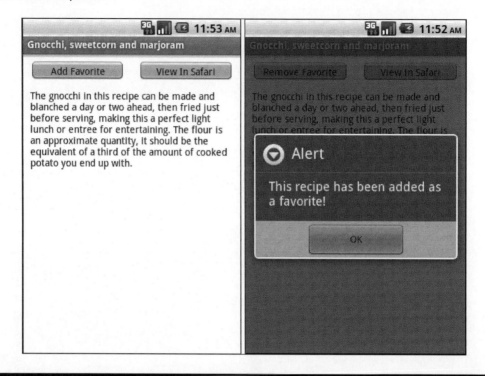

Retrieving data from an SQLite database

The ability to create a table and insert data into it is not of much use if we don't know how to retrieve that data and present it in some useful way to the user! We'll now introduce the concept of a **resultSet** (or recordSet if you prefer) in SQLite and how to retrieve data via this resultSet object that can be collected and returned to an array format suitable for usage within a TableView.

 Complete source code for this recipe can be found in the /Chapter 2/Recipe 8 folder.

How to do it...

In your `database.js` file, add the following function:

```
function getFavorites() {
  var sql = "SELECT * FROM favorites ORDER BY title ASC";
  var results = [];
  var resultSet = db.execute(sql);
  while (resultSet.isValidRow()) {
    results.push({
      id: resultSet.fieldByName('id'),
      title: resultSet.fieldByName('title'),
      description: resultSet.fieldByName('description'),
      link: resultSet.fieldByName('link')
    });

    //iterates to the next record
    resultSet.next();
  }

  //you must close the resultset
  resultSet.close();
  //finally, return our array of records!
  return results;
}
```

Now, open the `favorites.js` file for the first time, and type in the following code. Much of this code should be pretty familiar to you by now, including defining and adding a TableView to our Window, plus including the `database.js` file through our `Ti.include()` method.

```
Ti.include('database.js');
var win = Titanium.UI.currentWindow;

var data = []; //empty data array

var tblFavorites = Titanium.UI.createTableView({
  height: 366,
  width: 320,
  top: 0,
  left: 0
});
win.add(tblFavorites);
```

```
function loadFavorites(){
  data = []; //set our data object to empty
  data = getFavorites();
  tblFavorites.data = data;
}

//the focus event listener will ensure that the list
//is refreshed whenever the tab is changed
win.addEventListener('focus', loadFavorites);
```

How it works...

The first block of code is really just an extension of our previous recipe. But instead of creating or removing records, we are selecting them into a database recordset called "resultSet", and then looping through this resultSet object adding the data we require from each record into our `results` array.

The `results` array can then be added to our TableView's data property just like any other data source such as you obtained at the start of the chapter from an external XML feed. One thing to note is that you must *always* iterate to the new record in the resultSet using `resultSet.next()`, and when finished, *always close* the resultSet using `resultSet.close()`. A failure to do either of these actions can cause your application to record invalid data, leak memory badly, and in the worst case, fatally crash!

The previous screenshot shows the TableView in our **Favorites** tab displaying the records we have added as 'favorites' to our local SQLite database.

Creating a "pull and release" refresh mechanism

What happens if you want the user to be able to refresh the feed data in our table? You could create a regular button, or possibly check for new data at arbitrary time intervals. Alternatively, you could implement a cool 'pull and release' refresh mechanism made very popular by Twitter applications such as Tweetie and Twitter for Android.

In the final recipe for our **Recipe Finder** app, we will implement the very same type of refresh mechanism for our recipes feed, using the table view's `headerPullView` property.

 Complete source code for this recipe can be found in the `/Chapter 2/Recipe 9` folder, while the complete source code for this entire chapter can be found in the `/Chapter 2/RecipeFinder` folder.

How to do it...

Open your `recipes.js` file and type in the following code under the `"Ti.include"` statements. This is where will be creating the pull view and adding our user interface components to it, before creating the event listeners that will perform the data request.

```
//this variable defines whether the user is currently pulling
//the refresh mechanism or not
var pulling = false;

//defines whether we're currently fetching data or not
var reloading = false;

//let's create our 'pull to refresh' view
var tableHeader = Ti.UI.createView({
  backgroundImage: 'images/header.png',
  width:320,
  height:81
});

var arrowImage = Ti.UI.createView({
  backgroundImage:"images/arrow-down.png",
  width: 40,
```

```
    height: 40,
    bottom: 20,
    left:20
});

var statusLabel = Ti.UI.createLabel({
  text:"Pull to refresh...",
  left:85,
  width:200,
  bottom:28,
  height:"auto",
  color:"#000",
  textAlign:"center",
  font:{fontSize:20,fontWeight:"bold"},
  shadowColor:"#999",
  shadowOffset:{x:0,y:1}
});

var actInd = Titanium.UI.createActivityIndicator({
  left:20,
  bottom:20,
  width: 40,
  height: 40
});

tableHeader.add(actInd);
tableHeader.add(arrowImage);
tableHeader.add(statusLabel);

//define our table view
var tblRecipes = Titanium.UI.createTableView({
  height: 366,
  width: 320,
  top: 0,
  left: 0,
  rowHeight: 70,
  search: searchBar,
  filterAttribute:'filter' //here is the search filter which
                           //appears in TableViewRow
});
```

```
//add the header pull view
tblRecipes.headerPullView = tableHeader;

tblRecipes.addEventListener('scroll',function(e)
{
  var offset = e.contentOffset.y;
  if (offset <= -80.0 && !pulling)
  {
    pulling = true;
    arrowImage.backgroundImage = 'images/arrow-up.png';
    statusLabel.text = "Release to refresh...";
  }
  else if (pulling && offset > -80.0 && offset < 0)
  {
    pulling = false;
    arrowImage.backgroundImage = 'images/arrow-down.png';
    statusLabel.text = "Pull to refresh...";
  }
});
tblRecipes.addEventListener('scrollEnd',function(e)
{
  if (pulling && !reloading && e.contentOffset.y <= -80.0)
  {
    reloading = true;
    pulling = false;
    arrowImage.hide();
    actInd.show();
    statusLabel.text = "Reloading recipes...";
    tblRecipes.setContentInsets({top:80},{animated:true});

    //null out the existing recipe data
    tblRecipes.data = null;
    data = [];

    //open up the recipes xml feed
    xhr.open('GET', 'http://query.yahooapis.com/v1/public/
yql?q=select%20*%20from%20feed%20where%20url%3D%22http%3A%2F%2Fwww.
cuisine.com.au%2Ffeed%2Fall-recipes%22&format=json&diagnostics=fal
se');

    //and fetch it again
    xhr.send();
  }
});
```

Finally, in your `xhr.open()` method, we will do a check to see if this is the first time we're loading data or whether this is a reload call made by our "pull and release" mechanism. If it's the latter, we'll hide the header pull view and reset the contents of it back to its original state.

```
//check to see if we are refreshing the data via our
//pull and release mechanism
if(reloading == true){
   //when done, reset the header to its original style
   tblRecipes.setContentInsets({top:0},{animated:true});
   reloading = false;
   statusLabel.text = "Pull to refresh...";
   actInd.hide();
   arrowImage.backgroundImage = 'images/arrow-down.png';
   arrowImage.show();
}
```

How it works...

What we are doing here can really be broken up into two main components. First, we're creating a header view using standard UI components. Second, we're using events to know when our header view has been 'pulled' down far enough so that we can perform a refresh on our recipes data from the XML/JSON feed.

We know how far the header view has been pulled down via the `contentOffset` property of our TableView. In this case, we are executing the refresh of the data when the content offset hits 80px, which is the height of both the header view and also the height of the TableView's data rows from the top of the screen.

Finally, the two variables called `pulling` and `reloading` are used in conjunction so we can determine the series of steps in our "pull and release" refresh mechanism programmatically:

1. When the TableView is being pulled down by the user, using a tap and hold gesture (`pulling` = true)

2. When the TableView has finished pulling but has not yet started to reload the data from our remote data source (`pulling` = true and `reloading` = false)

3. When our pulling has completed but we are waiting for the data to finish being returned from our remote data source (`pulling` = false and `reloading` = true)

4. Finally, when our remote data source has finished streaming the required data and the header pull view can be closed, and the scrolling offset of our table can return to normal (`pulling = false` and `reloading = false`)

3
Integrating Google Maps and GPS

In this chapter, we will cover:

▸ Adding a MapView to your application

▸ Getting your current position with Geolocation

▸ Converting addresses to latitude and longitude positions

▸ Adding annotations to your MapView

▸ Customizing annotations and capturing MapView events

▸ Monitoring your heading using the device compass

▸ Drawing routes on your MapView

Introduction

Applications that utilize maps and location-based technology are second only to games and entertainment in sheer numbers of users and downloads on the iTunes store. This popularity with consumers is no surprise considering the multitude of uses we have found for them so far. From apps that help us navigate in the car and on foot, to being able to find a coffee shop or restaurant close by, the uses of this technology are truly only just being explored.

Titanium exposes the building blocks of this technology for us through the tight integration of Google Maps and GPS-based services for both the iPhone and the Android platform. Built-in geo-location, reverse geo-location and point-to-point routing are accessible all through Titanium's native API set. With these tools at your disposal, you can build anything from a store location finder to augmented reality applications.

Throughout the course of this chapter, we will introduce all of these core mapping concepts and use them to put together an exercise tracker app which will access our location at certain points and provide us feedback on how far we have traveled.

Pre-requisites

You should already be familiar with Titanium basics, including creating UI objects and using Titanium Studio. Additionally, it would be useful to have a basic understanding of how latitude and longitude positioning works, which is the standardized method of calculating the position of a person or object anywhere on Earth.

Adding a MapView to your application

Maps have become ubiquitous throughout all levels of technology. We now have real-time maps available everywhere from our computers, to our cars, the Web, and of course mobile devices. Google Maps is the most common platform implementation and the one both Android and the iPhone platforms utilize. In our first recipe for this chapter, we'll be implementing a MapView, and providing it with regional co-ordinates in the form of longitude and latitude values.

If you are intending to follow the entire chapter and build the **Exercise Tracker** app, then pay careful attention to the first *Getting ready* section for this recipe, as it will guide you through setting up the project.

Getting ready

To prepare for this recipe, open up Titanium Studio and log in if you have not already done so. If you need to register a new account, you can do so for free directly from within the application. Once you are logged in, click on **New Project**, and the details window for creating a new project will appear. Enter in `Exercise Tracker` as the name of the app, and fill in the rest of the details with your own information.

 Pay attention to the app identifier, which is written normally in reverse domain notation (that is *com.packtpub.exercisetracker*). This identifier cannot be easily changed after the project is created and you will need to match it *exactly* when creating provisioning profiles for distributing your apps later on.

Complete source code for this recipe can be found in the `/Chapter 3/Recipe 1` folder, while complete source code for this entire chapter can be found in the `/Chapter 3/Exercise Tracker` folder.

How to do it...

Our project has now been created using Titanium Studio. Let's get down to business! Open up the `app.js` file in your editor and remove all existing code. After you have done that, type in the following and then hit save:

```
//create the window
var win1 = Titanium.UI.createWindow({
  title:'Exercise Tracker',
  backgroundColor: '#000'
});

//create our mapview
var mapview = Titanium.Map.createView({
  top: 110,
  height: 350,
  mapType: Titanium.Map.STANDARD_TYPE,
  region: {latitude: 51.50015,
    longitude:-0.12623,
    latitudeDelta:0.5,
    longitudeDelta:0.5},
  animate: true,
  regionFit: true,
  userLocation: true
});

//add the map to the window
win1.add(mapview);

//finally, open the window
win1.open();
```

Try running the emulator now for either Android or iPhone. You should see a map appear in the bottom two-thirds of the screen, and after a few seconds it should center on London, England, as shown in the following screenshot. You may also receive a request at this point from the emulator asking if it can use your location. If this appears on your screen, simply select *yes*.

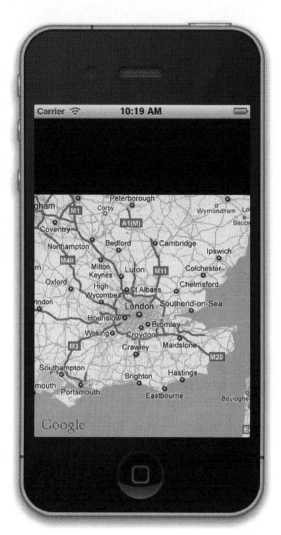

How it works...

Most of this code should be pretty familiar to you by now. We have created a `Window` object and added another object of type MapView to that window, before opening it via the `win1.open()` method. The MapView itself has a number of new properties that are relevant and significant only to it. These include:

- ▶ `region`: The region property accepts an array of parameters, which contain the latitude and longitude points that we wish to center the map on, as well as latitude and longitude delta values. The delta values indicate the zoom level of the map according to its centered location.

- ▶ `userLocation`: This Boolean value will turn on or off the blue *dot* indicator (an arrow on Android devices), which indicates where you are in relation to the MapView. It's important to note that this will probably not function in the emulator due to its inability to properly ascertain your current position.

- ▶ `animate`: This Boolean value will turn zooming and movement animation on or off in the MapView. Useful in the event of targeting older devices with low processing power and/or low bandwidth.

- ▶ `regionFit`: A Boolean that indicates whether the selected region fits the view dimensions given.

There's more...

After adding the Map view to your application, let's look at how we can make changes to the MapView's style.

Changing your MapView's style

There are actually a number of different MapView types you can add to your application, all accessible via the `TITANIUM.MAP` enumerator. The full set of map types available are as follows:

- ▶ `TITANIUM.MAP.STANDARD_TYPE`
- ▶ `TITANIUM.MAP.SATELLITE_TYPE`
- ▶ `TITANIUM.MAP.HYBRID_TYPE`

Getting your current position using GeoLocation

Our map may be working, but it is currently hardcoded to appear above London, England, and not all of us merry chaps work for Her Majesty. One of the great things about mapping technology is that we can determine our location from anywhere in the world via GPS satellites and, when GPS fails, mobile tower signals. This allows us to put maps into context, and let's you issue data to your user that is targeted to their environment.

In order to get our current location, we need to use the `Titanium.Geolocation` namespace, which contains a method called `getCurrentPosition`. The next recipe will explain how to use this namespace to adjust the bounds of our MapView to our current location.

 Complete source code for this recipe can be found in the `/Chapter 3/Recipe 2` folder.

How to do it...

Add in the following code after you have added your MapView component to the window:

```
//set the distance filter
Titanium.Geolocation.distanceFilter = 10;

//apple now requires this parameter so it can inform the user //of why
you are accessing their location data
Ti.Geolocation.purpose = "To obtain user location for tracking
distance travelled.";

Titanium.Geolocation.getCurrentPosition(function(e)
{
  if (e.error)
  {
    //if mapping location doesn't work, show an alert
    alert('Sorry, but it seems geo location
    is not available on your device!');
    return;
  }

  //get the properties from Titanium.GeoLocation
  var longitude = e.coords.longitude;
  var latitude = e.coords.latitude;
  var altitude = e.coords.altitude;
```

```
var heading = e.coords.heading;
var accuracy = e.coords.accuracy;
var speed = e.coords.speed;
var timestamp = e.coords.timestamp;
var altitudeAccuracy = e.coords.altitudeAccuracy;

//apply the lat and lon properties to our mapview
mapview.region = {latitude: latitude,
  longitude: longitude,
  latitudeDelta:0.5,
  longitudeDelta:0.5
};

});
```

Run your app in the emulator now and you should have a screen appear that looks similar to the following screenshot. Note that if you run the code in the emulator, the map will zoom to your current location but will not show the blue dot indicating your current location. You will need to run the application on a device in order to see the full results of this recipe.

How it works...

Getting our current position is simply a matter of calling the `getCurrentPosition` method of the `Titanium.Geolocation` namespace, and capturing the properties returned when this event fires. All of the information we need is then accessible via the `coords` property of the event object `(e)`. In the source code mentioned in the previous example, we have set a number of these properties to variables, some of which we will use in our Exercise Tracker application later on. Finally, we have taken the latitude and longitude properties from the `coords` object and reset the MapView's `region` according to these new values. The distance filter property being set determines how accurate you want your GPS location/position to be. In our case, we have set it to 10 meters, which is accurate enough for our purposes.

An important note for iPhone applications...

The second line in our block of code is a new requirement from Apple. It states that you must define exactly why you are requesting a user's location. This is there for your user's privacy and safety, so don't forget to add this line whenever you are using Geolocation, or Apple will probably reject your app from the iTunes store!

Converting addresses to latitude and longitude positions

Getting our location is all well and good when it's done for us, but humans don't think of places in terms of latitude and longitude values, we use good old addresses to define points on a map. To convert addresses to latitude and longitude decimal values, we can again use the `Titanium.Geolocation` namespace, and specifically a method in it called `forwardGeocoder`. Titanium has built-in methods for geo-coding, which utilize and essentially "black box" the services provided by the Google Maps API. The Google Geocoding API processes the converting addresses (such as "1600 Amphitheatre Parkway, Mountain View, CA") into geographic coordinates (for example, latitude: 37.423021 and longitude: 122.083739), which you can use to place markers or position the map. The Google Geocoding API provides a direct way to access a geocoder via an HTTP request.

Complete source code for this recipe can be found in the `/Chapter 3/Recipe 3` folder.

How to do it...

First, we need to create some input fields so that the user can provide us with a starting and an ending address. Let's create a new View and add it to the top of our window above the `MapView`. We'll also need to add a button to fire off the `forwardGeocoder` conversion. The background gradient image for the View is available within the `images` folder of the source code:

```
//create the search view
var searchview = Titanium.UI.createView({
  top: 0,
  left: 0,
  width: 320,
  height: 110,
  backgroundImage: 'images/gradient.png'
});

//style it up a bit
var bottomBorder = Titanium.UI.createView({
  height: 1,
  width: 320,
  left: 0,
  bottom: 0,
  backgroundColor: '#000'
});
searchview.add(bottomBorder);

//add a search box for starting location
var txtStartLocation = Titanium.UI.createTextField({
  backgroundColor: '#fff',
  left: 10,
  top: 20,
  width: 200,
  height: 30,
  borderColor: '#000',
  borderRadius: 5,
  hintText: 'Current Location',
  paddingLeft: 10
});
searchview.add(txtStartLocation);

//add a search box for starting location
var txtEndLocation = Titanium.UI.createTextField({
  backgroundColor: '#fff',
```

```
    left: 10,
    top: 60,
    width: 200,
    height: 30,
    borderColor: '#000',
    borderRadius: 5,
    hintText: 'End Location',
    paddingLeft: 10
});
searchview.add(txtEndLocation);

//add the button with an empty click event, this will fire off
//our forwardGeocoder
var btnSearch = Titanium.UI.createButton({
    width: 80,
    height: 30,
    top: 60,
    right: 10,
    backgroundImage: 'images/search.png',
    borderRadius: 3
});

//btnsearch event listener fires on button tap
btnSearch.addEventListener('click',function(e){

});
searchview.add(btnSearch);
```

Now, as we have some input fields, let's use the search button to capture those addresses and convert them into location values that we can use to define the region of our `MapView`. Put the next block of code into your button's `click` event handler:

```
//btnsearch event listener fires on button tap
btnSearch.addEventListener('click',function(e){

    //check for a start address
    if(txtStartLocation.value != '')
    {
        //works out the start co-ords
        Ti.Geolocation.forwardGeocoder(txtStartLocation.value, function(e)
{
            //we'll set our map view to this initial region so it
            //appears on screen
            mapview.region = {latitude: e.latitude,
                longitude: e.longitude,
```

```
        latitudeDelta:0.5,
        longitudeDelta:0.5
      };

      Ti.API.info('Start location co-ordinates are: ' +
      e.latitude + ' lat, ' + e.longitude +
      'lon');
    });
  }
  else
  {
    alert('You must provide a start address!');
  }

  //check for an end address
  if(txtEndLocation.value != '')
  {

    //do the same and work out the end co-ords
    Ti.Geolocation.forwardGeocoder(txtEndLocation.value, function(e){
      Ti.API.info('End location co-ordinates are: ' + e.latitude + '
lat, ' + e.longitude + ' lon');
    });
  }
  else
  {
    alert('You must provide an end address!');
  }

});
```

Run your app in the emulator and provide a start and an end address, and then hit **search**.
After a few seconds you should get the geolocation values of those addresses outputted
to the console, and your MapView should re-orientate itself to the region surrounding your
starting address. The following screenshot shows the start and end addresses converted to
latitude and longitude coordinates being outputted to the Titanium Studio console:

```
[INFO] Launching application in Simulator
[INFO] Launched application in Simulator (2.49 seconds)
[INFO] Application started
[INFO] ExerciseTracker/1.0 (1.6.0.9882e81)
[INFO] Start location co-ordinates are: -27.921040 lat,
153.333939 lon
[INFO] End location co-ordinates are: -27.627300 lat, 152.881027
lon
```

How it works...

The first section of code in this recipe is simple. Create a couple of TextFields for the start and end address and capture the click event of a Button component, wherein we pass those address values to our `Titanium.Geolocation.forwardGeocoder` method.

The forward geolocation task is actually performed against Google's servers. Titanium has wrapped this into one simple method for you to call, which saves you having to do the legwork of creating your own HTTP request against Google's server and then manually parsing the response.

You can try it out manually if you wish by reading the instructions at Google's own website: `http://code.google.com/apis/maps/documentation/geocoding/index.html`.

Adding annotations to your MapView

The ability to find locations on a map is extremely useful, but what the user needs is some kind of visual representation of that location on the screen. This is where annotations come in. In the next recipe, we will create annotation pins for both the start and end addresses, using the latitude and longitude values created by our `forwardGeocoder`.

 Complete source code for this recipe can be found in the `/Chapter 3/Recipe 4` folder.

How to do it...

Within your search button function and the `forwardGeocoder` method we called in the previous recipe, add the following code to create an annotation for the start location:

```
//works out the start co-ords
Ti.Geolocation.forwardGeocoder(txtStartLocation.value, function(e)
{
  //we'll set our map view to this initial region so it appears
  //on screen
  mapview.region = {latitude: e.latitude,
    longitude: e.longitude,
    latitudeDelta: 0.5,
    longitudeDelta: 0.5
  };

  Ti.API.info('Start location co-ordinates are: ' +
  e.latitude + ' lat, ' + e.longitude + ' lon');

  //add an annotation to the mapview for the start location
  var annotation = Titanium.Map.createAnnotation({
```

```
    latitude: e.latitude,
    longitude: e.longitude,
    title: 'Start location',
    subtitle: txtStartLocation.value,
    animate:true,
    id: 1,
    pincolor: Titanium.Map.ANNOTATION_GREEN
  });
  //add the annotation pin to the mapview
  mapview.addAnnotation(annotation);

});
```

Once you have added this code into the `forwardGeocoder` method for the start location, do exactly the same for your end location, except give the end location a `'myid'` property value of `2`. We will use these custom ID values later on when capturing events from our annotations; they will allow us to determine which annotation pin was tapped. Also, for your second annotation, give it a `pinColor` property of `Titanium.Map.ANNOTATION_RED`, as this well help distinguish the two pins on the map.

Load your application in the emulator and give it a start and an end location, then press **search**—you should end up with a couple of pins on your MapView, as shown in the following screenshot:

How it works...

Within your search button function and the `forwardGeocoder` method we called in the previous recipe, is the instantiation of a new object of type `annotation`, using `Titanium. Map.createAnnotation()`. This object represents a pin icon that is dropped onto the map to identify a specific location, and has a number of interesting properties. Apart from the standard longitude and latitude values, it can also accept a title and a secondary title, with the title being displayed more prominently at the top of the annotation and the secondary one below it. You should also give your annotations an `id` property (we have used `id` in this example), so that it is easier to identify them when you are adding events to your `MapView`. This is explained further in the next recipe.

Customizing annotations and capturing MapView events

Annotations can also be customized to give the user a better indication of what your location symbolizes. For example, if you were mapping restaurants in a particular area, you may provide each annotation with an icon that symbolized the type of restaurant it was—be it a pizza slice for Italian, a pint for pub food or a hamburger for a fast food chain.

In this recipe, we will add a left image to both the start and end location annotations, using an "S" (for "Start") and an "E" (for "End") icon respectively, to help the user identify them. We will also add a *start* button to the first pin, and a *stop* button to the second, which we will use to control our exercise timer later on.

 Complete source code for this recipe can be found in the /Chapter 3/Recipe 5 folder.

How to do it...

After your annotation is declared, but before it is added to your `mapView` object, type in the following code to create a custom `leftView` and custom `rightButton`. You should do the same for both the start location pin and the end location pin.

```
//add an image to the left of the annotation
var leftImage = Titanium.UI.createImageView({
    image: 'images/start.png',
    width: 25,
    height: 25
});
annotation.leftView = leftImage;
```

```
//add the start button
var startButton = 'images/startbutton.png';
annotation.rightButton = startButton;


mapview.addAnnotation(annotation);
```

Now, let's create the event listener for the `mapView` object. This function will execute when a user taps on any annotation in the map. You should place this code near the bottom of your JavaScript, just before the `mapView` is added to our window:

```
//create the event listener for when annotations
//are tapped on the map
mapview.addEventListener('click', function(e){
  Ti.API.info('Annotation id that was tapped: ' + e.source.id);
  Ti.API.info('Annotation button source that was tapped: ' +
e.clicksource);
});
```

How it works...

In this recipe, all we are doing at the beginning is pointing some new properties at each annotation. Our `leftView` is being populated by an `imageView`, using the image icons for "S" and "E" respectively. The annotation also accepts a simple URL string for the `rightButton` property, and it is here that we are providing the "start" and "stop" button image locations (both are to be found in the `images` folder of the source code).

The event listener for the `mapView` works slightly differently as compared to other event listeners. You need to capture an annotation click from the `mapView` parent object and then work out which annotation was tapped by means of a custom ID. In this case, we have used the `id` property to determine which annotation was the start location and which was the end location. The start location is set to `id 1`, while the end location is simply set to `id 2`.

Additionally, you may wish to perform different actions based on whether the right or left button on the annotation pin was tapped. We can determine this by using the event property's `(e) clicksource`. A comparison to a string of either `leftButton` or `rightButton` will let you know which was tapped and you can program functions into your app accordingly.

Drawing routes on your MapView

In order to track our movements and draw a route on the map, we need to create an array of points, each with its own latitude and longitude value. The MapView will take in this array of points as a property called route, and draw a series of lines to provide a visual representation of the route to the user.

In this recipe, we will create a timer that records our location every minute, and adds it to the points array. When each new point is recorded, we will access the Google Directions API to determine the distance and add that to our overall tally of how far we have traveled.

> Note that this recipe will not work on Android devices, as there is currently no support for Android routing in Titanium. However, it will work as described here for the iPhone and iPod Touch. There is an unsupported method of routing in Android, which you can read about at `http://bit.ly/pUq2v2`. You will need to use an actual iPhone or iPod Touch device to test this recipe, as the emulator will not be able to get your current location.

Complete source code for this recipe can be found in the `/Chapter 3/Recipe 6` folder.

How to do it...

Within your `mapView` click event, after the console logging to determine which button was tapped and which annotation, type in the following code:

```
//create the event listener for when annotations
//are tapped on the map
mapview.addEventListener('click', function(e){
  Ti.API.info('Annotation id that was tapped: ' + e.source.id);
  Ti.API.info('Annotation button source that was tapped: ' +
e.clicksource);
  Ti.API.info('Annotation button title that was tapped: ' + e.title);

  if(timerStarted == false && (e.clicksource == 'rightButton' &&
e.title == 'Start location'))
  {
    Ti.API.info('Timer will start...');
    points = [];

    //set our first point
    Ti.Geolocation.forwardGeocoder(txtStartLocation.value, function(e)
{
      points.push({latitude: e.coords.latitude,
        longitude: e.coords.longitude
      });
      route.points = points;
```

```
        //add route to our mapview object
        mapview.addRoute(route);

        timerStarted = true;

        //start our timer and refresh it every minute
        //1 minute = 60,000 milliseconds
        intTimer = setInterval(recordCurrentLocation,
        60000);
    });

  }
  else
  {
    //stop any running timer
    if(timerStarted == true &&
    (e.clicksource == 'rightButton'
    && e.title == 'End location'))
    {
      clearInterval(intTimer);
      timerStarted = false;
      alert('You travelled ' + distanceTraveled
      + ' meters!');
    }
  }
});
```

There are some variables we need to create now that need to be globally accessible to this JavaScript file. Add the following code to the very top of your `app.js` file:

```
//create the variables
var timerStarted = false;
var intTimer;

//this array will hold all the latitude and
//longitude points in our route
var points = [];

//this will hold the distance traveled
var distanceTraveled = 0;

//route object
var route = {
  name: 'Exercise Route',
  color: "#00f",
  width: 2
};
```

Next, we need to create the function for obtaining the user's new current location and determining how far the new location is from our previous location. Create this new function above the click event for the `mapView` component:

```
//this function records the current location and
//calculates distance between it and the last location,
//adding that to our overall distance count
function recordCurrentLocation()
{
  Ti.API.info('getting next position...');
  points.push({latitude:-27.466175,
    longitude:153.030426
  });
  route.points = points;

  //get the current position
  Titanium.Geolocation.getCurrentPosition(function(e) {
    var currLongitude = e.coords.longitude;
    var currLatitude = e.coords.latitude;
    points.push({latitude: e.currLatitude, longitude:
e.currLongitude});

    //add new point to route
    route.points = points;

    //remove the old route and add this new one
    mapview.removeRoute(route);
    mapview.addRoute(route);
  });

  //ask google for the distance between this point
  //and the previous point in the points[] array
  var url = 'http://maps.googleapis.com/maps/api/directions/json?tra
velMode=Walking&origin=' + points[points.length-2].latitude + ',' +
points[points.length-2].longitude + '&destination=' + points[points.
length-1].latitude + ',' + points[points.length-1].longitude +
'&sensor=false';
  var req = Ti.Network.createHTTPClient();
  req.open('GET', url);
  req.setRequestHeader('Content-Type', 'application/json;
charset=utf-8');
  req.onreadystate = function(){};
  req.onload = function()
  {
```

```
    //record the distance values
    Ti.API.info(req.responseText);
    var data = JSON.parse(req.responseText);
    Ti.API.info("distance.text " + data.routes[0].legs[0].distance.
text);
    Ti.API.info("distance.value " + data.routes[0].legs[0].distance.
value);
    distanceTraveled = distanceTraveled + data.routes[0].legs[0].
distance.value;
  };
  req.send();
}
```

How it works...

There are a number of things happening in this recipe, so let's break them down logically into their separate parts. First, we are obtaining the user's current location again on the start button's `click` event, and adding that as the first point in our `points` array. In order for our `mapView` component to use the array of point locations, we need to create a route object. This route object contains the array of points, plus the visual information such as the route's line, color, and thickness.

From there, we are creating a timer using `setInterval()`. This timer will only start when both the `timerStarted` variable is set to false, and when we can determine that the button tapped was indeed the right "start" button on one of our annotations.

Our timer is set to execute every 60 seconds, or as required by the code, 60,000 milliseconds. This means that every minute the function called `recordCurrentLocation()` will be executed. This function does the processing for determining our current location, and adds the new location to our "points" array. It then performs an HTTP request call to the Google APIs, which performs a distance calculation between our newest point, and the point location that we were at previously. This new distance is added to our total distance variable, called `distanceTraveled`.

Finally, whenever the user taps the *stop* button on the end annotation, the timer is stopped and the user is presented with an `alertDialog` showing the total value for how far they have traveled in meters. The following screenshot shows the route being drawn from our start to end location, and then the alert with the distance traveled when the *stop* button is tapped.

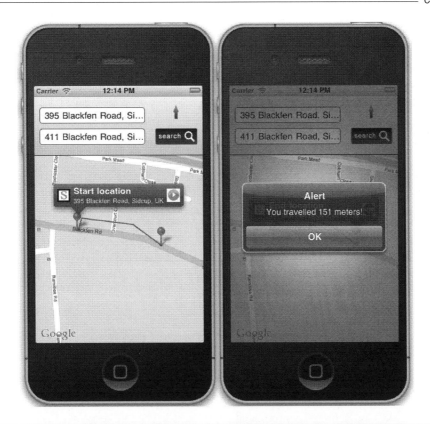

Monitoring your heading using the device compass

In this recipe, our final recipe for our chapter on Maps and GPS, we will be using the inbuilt device compass to determine your heading. We'll present that heading using an image of an arrow to represent the direction visually.

Note that this recipe will not work on older iPhone devices, such as the iPhone 3G, which lack the compass. You will need to use an actual device to test this recipe, as the emulator will not be able to get your current heading either.

Complete source code for this recipe can be found in the /Chapter 3/Recipe 7 folder.

Complete source code for the Exercise Tracker application built in this chapter can be found in the /Chapter 3/Exercise Tracker folder.

How to do it...

Add the following code to your `app.js` file, just before you perform a `win1.open()` method call at the end of the file:

```
//this image will appear over the map and indicate our
//current compass heading
var imageCompassArrow = Titanium.UI.createImageView({
    image: 'images/arrow.gif',
    width: 50,
    height: 50,
    right: 25,
    top: 5
});
win1.add(imageCompassArrow);

//how to monitor your heading using the compass
if(Titanium.Geolocation.hasCompass)
{
    //this is the degree of angle change our heading
    //events don't fire unless this value changes
    Titanium.Geolocation.headingFilter = 90;

    //this event fires only once to get our intial
    //heading and to set our compass "arrow" on screen
    Ti.Geolocation.getCurrentHeading(function(e) {
        if (e.error) {
        return;
    }
    var x = e.heading.x;
    var y = e.heading.y;
    var z = e.heading.z;
    var magneticHeading = e.heading.magneticHeading;
    accuracy = e.heading.accuracy;
    var trueHeading = e.heading.trueHeading;
    timestamp = e.heading.timestamp;

    var rotateArrow = Titanium.UI.create2DMatrix();
    var angle = 360 - magneticHeading;
    rotateArrow = rotateArrow.rotate(angle);
    imageCompassArrow.transform = rotateArrow;
});
```

```
//this event will fire repeatedly depending on the change
//in angle of our heading filter
Titanium.Geolocation.addEventListener('heading',function(e) {
  if (e.error) {
    return;
  }
  var x = e.heading.x;
  var y = e.heading.y;
  var z = e.heading.z;
  var magneticHeading = e.heading.magneticHeading;
  accuracy = e.heading.accuracy;
  var trueHeading = e.heading.trueHeading;
  timestamp = e.heading.timestamp;

  var rotateArrow = Titanium.UI.create2DMatrix();
  var angle = 360 - magneticHeading;
  rotateArrow = rotateArrow.rotate(angle);
  imageCompassArrow.transform = rotateArrow;
  });
}
else
{
  //log an error to the console if this device has no compass
  //older devices such as the iphone 3g don't have this
  Titanium.API.info("No Compass on device");

  //you can uncomment this to test rotation when using the emulator
  //var rotateArrow = Titanium.UI.create2DMatrix();
  //var angle = 45;
  //rotateArrow = rotateArrow.rotate(angle);
  //imageCompassArrow.transform = rotateArrow;
}
```

How it works...

We are first creating an `imageView` and setting its image property to our arrow image.
Initially, this will face towards the top of the screen, and will indicate north. This `imageView`
is then added to our `Window` object. The heading source code for this recipe is performing
two similar tasks: one gets our *initial* heading and the second fires on set intervals to get
our *current* heading. When the heading is obtained for either the current position or the new
position, we use the `magneticHeading` property to determine the angle (direction) in which
we are facing, and use a simple transformation to rotate the arrow in that direction.

Don't worry if you don't understand what a 2D matrix is, or how the transformation is performing the rotation of our image! We will be covering transformations, rotations, and animations in *Chapter 7, Creating Animations, Transformations and Understanding Drag-and-Drop*.

4
Enhancing your Apps with Audio, Video, and the Camera

In this chapter, we will cover:

- ▶ Choosing your capture device using an OptionDialog
- ▶ Capturing photos from the camera
- ▶ Choosing existing photos from the photo library
- ▶ Displaying photos using ScrollableView
- ▶ Saving your captured photo to the device filesystem
- ▶ Capturing and playing audio via the audio recorder
- ▶ Capturing video via the video recorder
- ▶ Playing video files from the filesystem
- ▶ Safely deleting saved files from the filesystem

Introduction

While it may be hard to believe, snapping photographs and sharing them wirelessly using a phone first happened only in 1997, and wasn't popularized until around 2004. By 2010, almost all phones contained a digital camera and many mid-range to high-end devices also sported audio and video camcorder capabilities. Most iPhone and Android models now have these capabilities, and they have opened new pathways for entrepreneurial developers.

Titanium contains APIs that let you access all of the phone interfaces required to take photos or video with the built-in camera, record audio, and scroll through the device's saved image and video galleries.

Throughout this chapter we will introduce all of these concepts and use them to put together a basic "Holiday Memories" app which will allow our users to capture photographs, videos, and audio from their device, save those files to the local file storage, and read them back again.

Pre-requisites

You should already be familiar with Titanium basics, including creating UI objects and using Titanium Studio. Additionally, to test camera functionality you are going to need either an iPhone or Android device capable of both recording photographs and video. An iPhone 3GS model or up will suffice, and all Android phones apart from the very bottom-end of the market should be OK.

Choosing your capture device using an OptionDialog

The OptionDialog is a modal-only component that allows you to show one or more options to a user, usually along with a *cancel* option, which closes the dialog. We are going to create this component and use it to present the user with an option to choose an image from the camera or the device's photo library.

If you are intending to follow the entire chapter and build the Holiday Memories app, then pay careful attention to the first *Getting ready* section for this recipe, as it will guide you through setting up the project.

Getting ready

To prepare for this recipe, open up Titanium Studio and log in if you have not already done so. If you need to register a new account, you can do so for free directly from within the application. Once you are logged in, click on **New Project**, and the details window for creating a new project will appear. Enter in **Holiday Memories** as the name of the app, and fill in the rest of the details with your own information.

Pay attention to the app identifier, which is written normally in reverse domain notation (that is *com.packtpub.holidaymemories*). This identifier cannot be easily changed after the project is created and you will need to match it *exactly* when creating provisioning profiles for distributing your apps later on. You can obtain all of the images used in this recipe, and indeed the entire chapter, by downloading the following source files:

Complete source code for this recipe can be found in the
/Chapter 4/Recipe 1 folder.

Complete source code for this entire chapter can be found in the
/Chapter 4/Holiday Memories folder.

How to do it...

Now our project has been created using Titanium Studio. Let's get down to business! Open up
the app.js file in your editor and remove all existing code. After you have done that, type in
the following and then hit save:

```
//this sets the background color of the master UIView (when there are
no windows/tab groups on it)
Titanium.UI.setBackgroundColor('#000');

//create tab group
var tabGroup = Titanium.UI.createTabGroup();

//
//create base UI tab and root window
//
var win1 = Titanium.UI.createWindow({
  title:'Photos',
  backgroundImage: 'images/background.png',
  barColor: '#000',
  url: 'photos.js'
});
var tab1 = Titanium.UI.createTab({
  icon:'images/photos.png',
  title:'Photos',
  window:win1
});

//
//create tab and root window
//
var win2 = Titanium.UI.createWindow({
  title:'Video',
  backgroundImage: 'images/background.png',
  barColor: '#000'
});
var tab2 = Titanium.UI.createTab({
```

```
    icon:'images/movies.png',
    title:'Video',
    window:win2
});


//
//create tab and root window
//
var win3 = Titanium.UI.createWindow({
    title:'Audio',
    backgroundImage: 'images/background.png',
    barColor: '#000'
});
var tab3 = Titanium.UI.createTab({
    icon:'images/audio.png',
    title:'Audio',
    window:win3
});


//
//add tabs
//
tabGroup.addTab(tab1);
tabGroup.addTab(tab2);
tabGroup.addTab(tab3);


//open tab group
tabGroup.open();
```

Now we need to create our first Window's JavaScript file that we will call `photo.js`. Create this blank file in your `Resources` folder and open it in your IDE. Enter in the following code to create the "Choose Photo" button which will instantiate your OptionDialog:

```
var win = Titanium.UI.currentWindow;

//our dialog with the options of where to get an
//image from
var dialog = Titanium.UI.createOptionDialog({
    title: 'Choose an image source...',
    options: ['Camera','Photo Gallery', 'Cancel'],
    cancel:2
});


//add event listener
dialog.addEventListener('click',function(e) {
```

```
    Ti.API.info('You selected ' + e.index);
});

//choose a photo button
var btnGetPhoto = Titanium.UI.createButton({
   title: 'Choose'
});
btnGetPhoto.addEventListener('click', function(e){
   dialog.show();
});

//set the right nav button to our btnGetPhoto object
//note that we're checking the osname and changing the
//button location depending on if it's iphone/android
//this is explained further on in the "Platform Differences" chapter
if(Ti.Platform.osname == 'iphone') {
   win.rightNavButton = btnGetPhoto;
}
else {
   //add it to the main window because android does
   //not have 'right nav button'
   btnGetPhoto.right = 20;
   btnGetPhoto.top = 20;
   win.add(btnGetPhoto);
}
```

How it works...

The code in the first block of code is creating our Navigation view with tabs and windows, all of which has been covered in *Chapter 1, Building Apps using Native UI Components* and *Chapter 2, Working with Local and Remote Data Sources*. Our first tab and window use the *photo.js* file, the contents of which are visible here in our second block of code on the previous page.

The OptionDialog itself is created using the `Titanium.UI.createOptionDialog()` method and only requires a few simple parameters. The `title` parameter, in this case, appears at the top of your button options and is there to just give your user a brief message about what their chosen option will be used for. In our case, we're simply notifying them that we'll be using their chosen option to launch the appropriate image capture application. The options array is the important property here and contains all of the button selections you wish to present to the user. Note that we have also included a `cancel` item in our array, and there is a corresponding `cancel` property with the same index as part of our `createOptionDialog()`. This will draw the button style for cancel a little differently when our OptionDialog is presented on screen.

Finally, we added an event listener to our OptionDialog and we are outputting the chosen button index to the Titanium Studio console, using the `e.index` property. We will use this flag in our next recipe to launch either the camera or photo gallery depending on the user's selection. The OptionDialog shown next provides the user with two image source options:

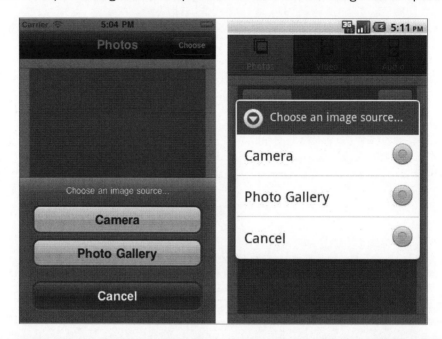

Capturing photos from the camera

To use the device camera we need to access the `Titanium.Media` namespace, and specifically the `showCamera` method. This will display the native operating system interface for taking photographs, and expose the three events which will help us decide what needs to be done with the captured image. We will also check whether the user's device is capable of taking camera shots before attempting to do so, as some devices (including iPod Touch and the emulator) don't have this capability.

Note that this recipe will only work if you are using a physical device! The emulators for both Android and the iPhone don't have camera functionality built in. If you attempt to run this on the emulator you will just be presented with an error dialog.

Complete source code for this recipe can be found in the `/Chapter 4/Recipe 2` folder.

How to do it...

We are going to extend the event listener of our OptionDialog using the following code:

```
//add event listener
dialog.addEventListener('click',function(e)
{
  Ti.API.info('You selected ' + e.index);
  if(e.index == 0)
  {
    //from the camera
    Titanium.Media.showCamera({
      success:function(event)
      {
        var image = event.media;

        if(event.mediaType == Ti.Media.MEDIA_TYPE_PHOTO)
        {
          //set image view
          var imgView =
          Titanium.UI.createImageView({
            top: 20,
            left: 20,
            width: 280,
            height: 320
          });
          imgView.image = image;
          win.add(imgView);
        }
      },
      cancel:function()
      {
        //getting image from camera was cancelled
      },
      error:function(error)
      {
        //create alert
        var a = Titanium.UI.createAlertDialog({title:'Camera'});

        // set message
        if (error.code == Titanium.Media.NO_CAMERA)
        {
```

```
            a.setMessage('Device does not have image recording
capabilities');
            }
        else
          {
          a.setMessage('Unexpected error: ' + error.code);
        }

        // show alert
        a.show();
      },
      allowImageEditing:true,
      saveToPhotoGallery:false
    });
  }
  else
  {
    //cancel was tapped
    //user opted not to choose a photo
  }
});
```

Run your app on a physical device now and you should be able to select the camera button from our OptionDialog and take a photograph with your device. This image should then appear in our temporary ImageView like it does in the following screenshot:

How it works...

Getting an image from the camera is actually pretty straightforward. First, you'll notice that we've extended the OptionDialog with an if statement. If the index property of our dialog is 0 (the first button) then we are launching the camera. We do this via the `Titanium.Media.showCamera()` method. This fires three events, which we are capturing here, called **success**, **error**, and **cancel**. We are ignoring the cancel event, as there is no processing required if the user opts to cancel out of the image capture. In the error event, we are going to display an AlertDialog that explains that the camera cannot be initiated. This is the dialog you will see if you happen to run this code using an emulator.

The majority of our processing takes place in the success event. First, we save the captured photograph into a new variable called `image`. We then check that the chosen media was actually a photograph by comparing its `mediaType` property. It is at this point that the chosen media could actually be a video, so we must double check what it is before we use it, as we don't know whether the user has taken a photo or video shot until after it has happened. Finally, to show that we have actually captured an image with our camera to the user, we create an ImageView and set its `image` property to the captured image file, before adding the entire thing to our window.

Choosing existing photos from the photo library

The process of choosing an image from the photo library on the device is very similar to that of the camera. We are still using the `Titanium.Media` namespace, however, this time we are going to execute the method called `openPhotoLibrary()`, which does exactly as the name suggests. As with the previous recipe, once we have retrieved an image from the Photo Gallery, we will display it on screen to the user using a simple ImageView control.

 Complete source code for this recipe can be found in the `/Chapter 4/Recipe 3` folder.

How to do it...

We are going to further extend our OptionDialog to now choose an image from the photo library, if the `index` property of 1 (the second button) is selected. Add the following code into your dialog's event listener:

```
//add event listener
dialog.addEventListener('click',function(e)
{
```

```
        Ti.API.info('You selected ' + e.index);
    if(e.index == 1)
    {
      //obtain an image from the gallery
      Titanium.Media.openPhotoGallery({

        success:function(event)
        {
          var image = event.media;

          // set image view
          Ti.API.debug('Our type was: '+event.mediaType);
          if(event.mediaType == Ti.Media.MEDIA_TYPE_PHOTO)
          {
            var imgView = Titanium.UI.createImageView({
              top: 20,
              left: 20,
              width: 280,
              height: 320
            });

            imgView.image = image;
            win.add(imgView);
          }
        },
        cancel:function()
        {
          //user cancelled the action from within
          //the photo gallery
        }
      });
    }
    else
    {
      //cancel was tapped
      //user opted not to choose a photo
    }
});
```

Run your app in the emulator or device and choose the second option from our dialog. The photo library should appear and allow you to select an image. This selection screen will look something like the following screenshot:

How it works...

This recipe follows more or less the same pattern as when we used the camera to obtain our image. First, we extended the OptionDialog event listener to perform an action when the button index selected equals 1, which in this case is our Photo Gallery button. Our openPhotoGallery() method also fires three events: **success**, **error**, and **cancel**.

Just like the previous recipe, the majority of our processing takes place in the success event. We check that the chosen media was actually a photograph by comparing its mediaType property, and finally we create an ImageView and set its image property to the captured image file, before adding the entire thing to our window.

There's more...

Now, let's explore media types.

Understanding Media Types

There are two main media types available to you via the `mediaType` enumeration when capturing photographs or videos via the in-built camera. These are:

- ▸ `MEDIA_TYPE_PHOTO`
- ▸ `MEDIA_TYPE_VIDEO`

In addition, there are also numerous other sets of more specific `mediaType`'s in the enumeration, which include the following:

- ▸ `MUSIC_MEDIA_TYPE_ALL`
- ▸ `MUSIC_MEDIA_TYPE_ANY_AUDIO`
- ▸ `MUSIC_MEDIA_TYPE_AUDIOBOOK`
- ▸ `MUSIC_MEDIA_TYPE_MUSIC`
- ▸ `MUSIC_MEDIA_TYPE_PODCAST`
- ▸ `VIDEO_MEDIA_TYPE_AUDIO`
- ▸ `VIDEO_MEDIA_TYPE_NONE`
- ▸ `VIDEO_MEDIA_TYPE_VIDEO`

These types are generally only applicable when utilizing the `mediaType` property from within the `VideoPlayer` or `AudioPlayer` components.

Saving to photos

You can run this code in the emulator, but you'll probably notice that there are no images in the library and no obvious way to get them there! Thankfully, this is actually fairly easy to overcome. Simply open the web browser and find an image you want to test with using Google Images or a similar service. Click and hold on an image in the browser and you should see an option **save to photos**. You can then use these images to test out your code in the emulator.

Displaying photos using ScrollableView

One of the most common methods of displaying multiple photographs and images on mobile devices is the `ScrollableView`. This view type allows for pictures to be swiped left and right, and is common among many applications including Facebook mobile. The method of showing images in this way is reminiscent of "flipping" through a book or album, and is very popular due to the natural feel and simple implementation.

In this recipe we will implement a `ScrollableView` which will contain any number of images that can be chosen from the camera or photo gallery. Complete source code for this recipe can be found in the `/Chapter 4/Recipe 4` folder.

> Note that this recipe should work for both Android and iPhone devices. However, a recent bug in the latest version of Titanium SDK (1.7.2) may cause it to fail on Android. You should check whether you are using the latest version of Titanium SDK if you wish to test this on the Android emulator.

How to do it...

First, let's create our ScrollableView object, which we will call `scrollingView`, and add it to our `photo.js` window:

```
//this is the scroll view the user will use to swipe
//through the selected photos
scrollingView = Titanium.UI.createScrollableView({
  left: 17,
  top: 15,
  width: win.width - 14,
  height: win.height - 25,
  views: [],
  currentPage: 0,
  zIndex: 1
});

scrollingView.addEventListener('scroll',function(e){
  Ti.API.info('Current scrollableView page = ' + e.source.
currentPage);
});

win.add(scrollingView);
```

Now we are going to alter the dialog event listener in order to assign our selected photos to the ScrollableView, instead of the temporary ImageView we created earlier. Replace all of the code within and including your `if(event.mediaType == Ti.Media.MEDIA_TYPE_PHOTO)` with the following code. Note you need to do this for both the images gathered from the photo library and from the device camera.

```
. . .

//output the mediaType to the console log for debugging
Ti.API.debug('Our type was: '+event.mediaType);
```

```
if(event.mediaType == Ti.Media.MEDIA_TYPE_PHOTO)
{
  // set image view
  var imgView = Titanium.UI.createImageView({
    top: 0,
    left: 0,
    width: 286,
    height: 337,
    image: image
  });

  //add the imageView to our scrollableView object
  scrollingView.addView(imgView);

}
```

Now run your app in either the emulator or your device, and select a couple of images one after the other. You can use a combination of images from the camera or the photo gallery. Once you have selected at least two images, you should be able to swipe between them using a left-to-right or right-to-left gesture.

How it works...

The ScrollableView is really just a collection of views that has a number of special events and properties built into it, as you can probably tell by the empty array value we have given to the property called `views` in the `createScrollableView()` method. It is necessary to set this property on instantiating the ScrollableView object, and a good idea to set the `currentPage` index property to 0; our first view. We are still creating an ImageView as per the previous recipes. However, this time we are not adding that View to our window, but to our `ScrollableView` component. We do this by adding a view using the `addView()` method. Finally, we have also created an event that attaches to our ScrollableView called `scroll`, and we are outputting the `currentPage` property to the Titanium console for debugging and testing.

As you can see, the ScrollableView is an easy and simple component and is very useful for photo gallery applications or any other apps where you want to display a series of similar views. You could extend this by adding a blank View object and putting any number of text fields, labels, or image views you want in each of those blank views—the only limit here is your imagination!

Saving your captured photo to the device filesystem

Taking pictures is all well and good, but what about when we wish to save an image to the filesystemso we can retrieve it again later? In this recipe we will do exactly that and also introduce you to the `toImage()` method which is inbuilt in many of the Titanium controls. This method takes a flattened image of the entire view it is called upon and is extremely useful for taking screenshots or grabbing an image of many controls lumped together in a single view.

 Complete source code for this recipe can be found in the `/Chapter 4/Recipe 5` folder.

How to do it...

Type in the following code after your btnGetPhoto object is created. You can replace the existing code that we've written to add the btnGetPhoto object to the navigation bar, as this code repeats that code and also extends it.

```
//save a photo to file system button
var btnSaveCurrentPhoto = Titanium.UI.createButton({
  title: 'Save Photo',
  zIndex: 2 //this appears over top of other components
});
btnSaveCurrentPhoto.addEventListener('click', function(e){
  var media = scrollingView.toImage();

  //if it doesn't exist, create it create a directory called
  //"photos"
  //and it will hold our saved images
  var newDir =
    Titanium.Filesystem.getFile
    (Titanium.Filesystem.applicationDataDirectory,'photos');
  if(!newDir.exists()){
    newDir.createDirectory();
  }

  var fileName = 'photo-' + scrollingView.currentPage.toString()
    + '.png';
  writeFile = Titanium.Filesystem.getFile(newDir.nativePath,
    fileName);
  writeFile.write(media);

  alert('You saved a file called ' + fileName +
    ' to the directory ' + newDir.nativePath);

  var _imageFile = Titanium.Filesystem.getFile(newDir.nativePath,
    fileName);
  if (!_imageFile.exists()) {
    Ti.API.info('ERROR: The file ' + fileName +
      ' in the directory ' + newDir.nativePath + ' does not exist!');
  }
  else {
    Ti.API.info('OKAY!: The file ' + fileName +
      ' in the directory ' + newDir.nativePath + ' does exist!');
  }
```

```
});

//set the right nav button to our photo get button
if(Ti.Platform.osname == 'iphone') {
  win.leftNavButton = btnSaveCurrentPhoto;
  win.rightNavButton = btnGetPhoto;
}
else
{
  //add it to the main window because android does
  //not have 'right nav button'
  btnGetPhoto.right = 20;
  btnGetPhoto.top = 20;
  win.add(btnGetPhoto);

  //add it to the main window because android does
  //not have 'left nav button'
  btnSaveCurrentPhoto.left = 20;
  btnSaveCurrentPhoto.top = 20;
  win.add(btnSaveCurrentPhoto);
}
```

How it works...

The `Titanium.FileSystem` namespace opens up a range of file manipulation capabilities, but most importantly, gives us the basic tools in order to read and write a file to the application's storage space on the device. In this recipe we are using the `toImage()` method of the `scrollingView` to return a blob of the view's image representation.

We can then get a reference to the folder we wish to store the image file data in. As you can see in the code, we are getting a reference to that folder by creating a new variable such as `var newDir = Titanium.Filesystem.getFile(Titanium.Filesystem.applicationDataDirectory, 'photos');` and then ensuring that the folder exists. If it doesn't exist, we can create the folder by calling the `createDirectory()` method on our `newDir` object.

Finally, our image data is saved in much the same way. First, we create a variable called `writeFile`, which is referencing our file name within the `newDir` object folder we have already created. We can then output the file to the filesystem using `writeFile`'s `"write()"` method, passing in the image media variable as the file data to save.

Capturing and playing audio via the audio recorder

Another handy feature of the iPhone and most Android handsets is the ability to record audio data—perfect for taking audible notes during meetings or those long, boring lectures! In this recipe we are going to capture some audio using the `Titanium.Media.AudioRecorder` class, and then allow the user to play back the recorded sound file.

Complete source code for this recipe can be found in the `/Chapter 4/Recipe 6` folder.

 Note that this recipe will only work for the iPhone. You will also require a physical device for this recipe. Later versions of the Titanium framework should support audio recording for Android via the use of intents. In addition, the iPhone 3G models may not be capable of recording in some of the following compression formats, particularly high fidelity formats such as AAC. When in doubt, you should try using MP4A or WAV formats.

Getting ready

Create a new JavaScript file called `audio.js` and save it into your resources directory. Then back in your `app.js` file, add the URL property of window3, and give it a value of `audio.js`. This will load up our video JavaScript file for the third tab window of our application.

How to do it...

Type in the following code into your `audio.js` file and save. This will set up the interface with a set of buttons and labels so we can start, stop, and playback our recorded audio.

```
var win = Titanium.UI.currentWindow;

var file;
var timer;
var sound;
var duration = 0;


var label = Titanium.UI.createLabel({
  text:'',
  top:150,
  color:'#999',
  textAlign:'center',
  width: 250,
```

```
  height:'auto'
});

win.add(label);

var linetype = Titanium.UI.createLabel({
  text: "audio line type: "+lineTypeToStr(),
  bottom: 15,
  color:'#999',
  textAlign:'center',
  width: 250,
  height:'auto'
});

win.add(linetype);

var volume = Titanium.UI.createLabel({
  text: "volume: "+Ti.Media.volume,
  bottom:50,
  color:'#999',
  textAlign:'center',
  width: 250,
  height:'auto'
});

win.add(volume);


var switchLabel = Titanium.UI.createLabel({
  text:'Hi-fidelity:',
  width: 250,
  height:'auto',
  textAlign:'center',
  color:'#999',
  bottom:115
});

var switcher = Titanium.UI.createSwitch({
  value:false,
  bottom:80
});
```

```
win.add(switchLabel);
win.add(switcher);

var b2 = Titanium.UI.createButton({
  title:'Playback Recording',
  width:200,
  height:40,
  top:80
});
win.add(b2);

var b1 = Titanium.UI.createButton({
  title:'Start Recording',
  width:200,
  height:40,
  top:20
});
win.add(b1);
```

Now run your application in the emulator and switch to the **Audio** tab. You should see a screen that looks just like the following screenshot:

Now we're going to create an object instance of the `AudioRecorder` method called `recording`, and give it a compression value and format value. We will also add event listeners to watch out for when the volume, audio line, and recording properties change, along with event handlers to capture and process these changes. Type in the following directly after the code you created from the previous page:

```
var recording = Ti.Media.createAudioRecorder();

// default compression is Ti.Media.AUDIO_FORMAT_LINEAR_PCM
// default format is Ti.Media.AUDIO_FILEFORMAT_CAF

// this will give us a wave file with µLaw compression which
// is a generally small size and suitable for telephony //recording
for high end quality, you'll want LINEAR PCM –
//however, that will result in uncompressed audio and will be //very
large in size
recording.compression = Ti.Media.AUDIO_FORMAT_LINEAR_PCM;
recording.format = Ti.Media.AUDIO_FILEFORMAT_CAF;

Ti.Media.addEventListener('recordinginput', function(e) {
  Ti.API.info('Input availability changed: '+e.available);
  if (!e.available && recording.recording) {
    b1.fireEvent('click', {});
  }
});

Ti.Media.addEventListener('linechange',function(e)
{
  linetype.text = "audio line type: "+lineTypeToStr();
});

Ti.Media.addEventListener('volume',function(e)
{
  volume.text = "volume: "+e.volume;
});
```

Finally, add the section of code after your `Ti.Media` event listeners that you created previously. This code will handle all of the events for the audio input controls (the stop/start buttons and our high-fidelity switch).

```
function lineTypeToStr()
{
  var type = Ti.Media.audioLineType;
  switch(type)
  {
```

```
    case Ti.Media.AUDIO_HEADSET_INOUT:
      return "headset";
    case Ti.Media.AUDIO_RECEIVER_AND_MIC:
      return "receiver/mic";
    case Ti.Media.AUDIO_HEADPHONES_AND_MIC:
      return "headphones/mic";
    case Ti.Media.AUDIO_HEADPHONES:
      return "headphones";
    case Ti.Media.AUDIO_LINEOUT:
      return "lineout";
    case Ti.Media.AUDIO_SPEAKER:
      return "speaker";
    case Ti.Media.AUDIO_MICROPHONE:
      return "microphone";
    case Ti.Media.AUDIO_MUTED:
      return "silence switch on";
    case Ti.Media.AUDIO_UNAVAILABLE:
      return "unavailable";
    case Ti.Media.AUDIO_UNKNOWN:
      return "unknown";
  }
}


function showLevels()
{
  var peak = Ti.Media.peakMicrophonePower;
  var avg = Ti.Media.averageMicrophonePower;
  duration++;
  label.text = 'duration: '+duration+' seconds\npeak power:
    ' + peak +'\navg power: ' +avg;
}

b1.addEventListener('click', function()
{
  if (b1.title == "Stop Recording")
  {
    file = recording.stop();
    b1.title = "Start Recording";
    b2.show();
    clearInterval(timer);
    Ti.Media.stopMicrophoneMonitor();
  }
  else
  {
```

```
    if (!Ti.Media.canRecord) {
      Ti.UI.createAlertDialog({
        title:'Error!',
        message:'No audio recording hardware is currently
          connected.'
      }).show();
      return;
    }
    b1.title = "Stop Recording";
    recording.start();
    b2.hide();
    Ti.Media.startMicrophoneMonitor();
    duration = 0;
    timer = setInterval(showLevels,1000);
  }
});


b2.addEventListener('click', function()
{
  if (sound && sound.playing)
  {
    sound.stop();
    sound.release();
    sound = null;
    b2.title = 'Playback Recording';
  }
  else
  {
    Ti.API.info("recording file size: "+file.size);
    sound = Titanium.Media.createSound({sound:file});
    sound.addEventListener('complete', function()
    {
      b2.title = 'Playback Recording';
    });
    sound.play();
    b2.title = 'Stop Playback';
  }
});


switcher.addEventListener('change',function(e)
{
  if (!switcher.value)
  {
```

```
      recording.compression = Ti.Media.AUDIO_FORMAT_ULAW;
    }
    else
    {
      recording.compression = Ti.Media.AUDIO_FORMAT_LINEAR_PCM;
    }
});
```

Now run your application on a device (the simulator may not be capable of recording audio) and you should be able to start, stop, and then playback your audio recording, while the high fidelity switch will change the audio compression to a higher fidelity format.

How it works...

In this recipe we are creating an instance of the AudioRecorder object, and we have called this new object recording. We're giving this object a compression and audio format. For now, we have set these to the default (PCM compression and standard CAF format). Listeners from the Titanium.Media namespace are then added, which when fired will change the line type or volume labels respectively.

The main processing for this recipe happens within the event handlers for the "Start/Stop" and "Playback" buttons called b1 and b2 respectively. Our first button, b1, is first checking its title to determine whether to stop or start recording via a simple if statement. If recording has not started, then we kick off the process by calling the start method of our recording object. To do so, we also need to start the microphone monitor, which is done by executing the line Ti.Media.startMicrophoneMonitor(). Our device will then begin recording. Tapping the b1 button again will execute the stop code and simultaneously set our file object (the resulting sound-audio file) to the output from our recording object.

The b2 button event handler checks whether we have a valid sound file, and whether it is already playing. If we have a valid file and it's playing, then the playback will stop. Otherwise, if there is a valid sound file and it hasn't already been played back through the speaker, we are creating a new object called sound, using the Titanium.Media.createSound method. This method requires a sound parameter. We passed the file object to it that was created during our recording session. Executing the sound object's play method then kicks off the playback, while the event listener/handler for the playback completion resets our b2 button title when the playback has completed.

Finally, the switch (called switcher in this example) simply changes the recording format from high fidelity compression to a low one. The lower the quality and compression, the smaller the resulting audio file will end up being.

Capturing video via the video recorder

You can also use the inbuilt camera of your iPhone (3GS and above) or Android device to record video. The quality and length of the video that you can record is dependant on both your device's memory capabilities and the type of camera that's included in the hardware. However, you should at least be able to capture short video clips in VGA resolution as a minimum.

In this recipe we will create a basic interface for our **Video** tab consisting of a record button, which will launch the camera and record video on your device. We'll also perform this in two separate ways: using standard Titanium code for the iPhone and using intents for Android.

 Note that this recipe will require a physical device for testing. In addition, the iPhone 3G models are not be capable of recording video, but all models from the 3GS and upwards should be fine.

Getting ready

Create a new JavaScript file called `video.js` and save it into your resources folder. Then, back in your `app.js` file, add the URL property of window2 and give it a value of `video.js`. This will load up our video JavaScript file for the second tab window of our application.

 Complete source code for this recipe can be found in the `/Chapter 4/Recipe 7` folder.

How to do it...

First of all, let's set up the basic interface to have a record button (in the navigation bar section for the iPhone and as a normal button for Android), along with the `videoFile` variable. This will hold the path to our recorded video as a string.

```
var win = Titanium.UI.currentWindow;

var videoFile = 'video/video-test.mp4';

var btnGetVideo = Titanium.UI.createButton({
  title: 'Record Video'
});

//set the right nav butto to our get button
if(Ti.Platform.osname == 'iphone') {
```

```
        win.rightNavButton = btnGetVideo;
    }
    else {
        //add it to the main window because android does
        //not have 'right nav button'
        btnGetVideo.right = 20;
        btnGetVideo.top = 20;
        win.add(btnGetVideo);
    }
```

Now let's create the event listener and handler code for the record button. This will check our current platform (either iPhone or Android) and execute the record video code for the correct platform:

```
    //get video from the device
    btnGetVideo.addEventListener('click', function()
    {
        if(Titanium.Platform.osname == 'iphone') {
            //record for iphone
            Titanium.Media.showCamera({
                success:function(event)
                {
                    var video = event.media;
                    movieFile = Titanium.Filesystem.getFile(
                        Titanium.Filesystem.applicationDataDirectory,
                        mymovie.mov');

                    movieFile.write(video);
                    videoFile = movieFile.nativePath;
                    btnGetVideo.title = 'Play Video';
                },
                cancel:function()
                {
                },
                error:function(error)
                {
                    // create alert
                    var a =
                    Titanium.UI.createAlertDialog({title:'Video'});

                    // set message
                    if (error.code == Titanium.Media.NO_VIDEO)
                    {
                        a.setMessage('Device does not have video recording
                            capabilities');
```

```
      }
      else
      {
        a.setMessage('Unexpected error: ' + error.code);
      }

      // show alert
      a.show();
    },
    mediaTypes: Titanium.Media.MEDIA_TYPE_VIDEO,
    videoMaximumDuration:10000,
    videoQuality:Titanium.Media.QUALITY_HIGH
  });
}
else
{
  //record for android using intents
  var intent = Titanium.Android.createIntent({
    action: 'android.media.action.VIDEO_CAPTURE'
  });

  Titanium.Android.currentActivity.startActivityForResult(
    intent, function(e) {

      if (e.error) {
        Ti.UI.createNotification({
          duration: Ti.UI.NOTIFICATION_DURATION_LONG,
          message: 'Error: ' + e.error
        }).show();
      }
      else {

        if (e.resultCode === Titanium.Android.RESULT_OK) {
          videoFile = e.intent.data;
          var source = Ti.Filesystem.getFile(videoFile);
          movieFile =
          Titanium.Filesystem.getFile(
            Titanium.Filesystem.applicationDataDirectory,
          'mymovie.3gp');

          source.copy(movieFile.nativePath);
          videoFile = movieFile.nativePath;
          btnGetVideo.title = 'Play Video';
        }
```

```
        else {
          Ti.UI.createNotification({
            duration: Ti.UI.NOTIFICATION_DURATION_LONG,
            message: 'Canceled/Error? Result code: ' +
              e.resultCode
          }).show();
        }
      }
    });


  }
});
```

How it works...

Let's work through the code for recording on iPhone devices first, which is encapsulated within the `if(Titanium.Plaform.osname == 'iphone')` statement as mentioned in the previous code. Here, we are executing the camera in the same way you would for capturing plain photos, however, we're passing additional parameters. The first of these is called `mediaType`, and it tells the device we want to capture a `mediaType` of `MEDIA_TYPE_VIDEO`.

The other two parameters define how long and what quality to capture the video in. The parameter `videoMaximumDuration` float defines the duration (how long in milliseconds to allow capture before completing,) while the `videoQuality` constant indicates the video quality during capture. We have set these to 10 seconds (10,000 milliseconds) and a video quality of "high" respectively.

On successful video capture, we save the `event.media` (our video in its raw format) to the filesystem, using pretty much the same method as we did when saving a photograph. The final step is to set the `videoFile` path to the location of our newly saved video file on the filesystem.

For Android, we are capturing the video in a different way, using an *intent*. In this case, we're using the video capture intent called `android.media.action.VIDEO_CAPTURE`. Objects of type `android.content.Intent` are used to send asynchronous messages within your application or between applications. Intents allow the application to send or receive data to and from other activities or services. They also allow it to broadcast that a certain event has occurred. In our recipe's code, we are executing our Intent and then capturing the result—if the `resultCode` equals `Titanium.Android.RESULT_OK` then we know that we've managed to record a video clip. We can then move this file from its temporary storage location to a new destination of our choosing.

 Note that we are capturing video in 3GP format for Android while it was in MP4/MOV format on the iPhone.

Playing video files from the filesystem

Now that we have recorded video, what about playing it back? Titanium has an inbuilt video player component that can play both local files and remote video URLs. In this recipe we'll show you how to create the video player control and pass the local file URL of the video we captured in the previous recipe to it.

 Complete source code for this recipe can be found in the /Chapter 4/Recipe 8 folder.

How to do it...

In our videos.js file, underneath the declaration for the videoFile object, create the following function:

```
function playMovie(){
  //create the video player and add it to our window
  //note the url property can be a remote url or a local file
  var my_movie = Titanium.Media.createVideoPlayer({
    url: videoFile,
    width: 280,
    height: 200,
    top:20,
    left:20,
    backgroundColor:'#000'
  });

  win.add(my_movie);
  my_movie.play();
}
```

Then, in your event listener for btnGetVideo, extend the code so that it checks the button title and plays the recorded video when it has been saved:

```
//get video from the device
btnGetVideo.addEventListener('click', function()
{
  if(btnGetVideo.title == 'Record Video') {
    //our record video code from the previous recipe
    //...
  }
  else
```

```
      {
        playMovie();
      }
    });
```

How it works...

Creating a video player object is no different than creating Labels or Buttons as many of the same properties are utilized for positioning and layout. The player can be embedded into any other view as you would do with a normal control, meaning you could have video thumbnails playing directly from within the rows of a TableView if you wanted. Additionally, the Video Player can play both local and remote videos (using the Video `url` property). In this recipe, we are uploading a saved video from the filesystem that was captured by the camcorder on our device.

You could just as easily load a video from a URL or directly from within your `Resources` folder. There is a 10 second video attached to the source code for this chapter in both `mp4` and `3gp` formats for you to test with, called `video-test.mp4`. You can also attempt to load it remotely using the web address `http://boydlee.com/video-test.mp4`.

 Note that some web video formats such as FLV are not supported.

There's more...

If you want your video to play using the full screen dimensions and not just within a view, then you can set its `fullscreen` property to `true`. This will automatically load the video into fullscreen mode when it starts playing.

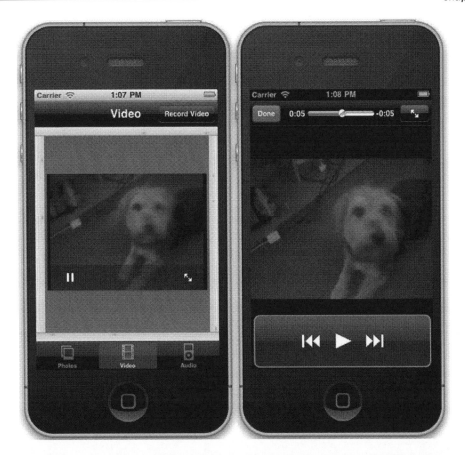

Safely deleting saved files from the filesystem

We can create these files and write them to our local phone storage, but what about deleting them? In this recipe we'll explain how to safely check for and delete files using the `Titanium.Filesystem.File` namespace.

 Complete source code for this recipe can be found in the `/Chapter 4/Recipe 9` folder.

How to do it...

Back in your `photos.js` file, add the following button code with an event listener at the end of the file. This will be our "trash" button and will call the delete function on the current selected image.

```
//create trash button
var buttonTrash = Titanium.UI.createButton({
  width: 25,
  height: 25,
  right: 25,
  bottom: 25,
  image: 'images/trash.jpg',
  zIndex: 2,
  visible: false
});
//create event listener for trash button
buttonTrash.addEventListener('click', function(e){

});
```

Add an extra line to our existing `btnSaveCurrentPhoto` click event to make our trash button visible only after a photo has actually been saved to the disk:

```
btnSaveCurrentPhoto.addEventListener('click', function(e){

    buttonTrash.visible = true;
});
```

Finally, extend your button's event listener to delete the file, only after making sure that it already exists, before adding our button to the window:

```
buttonTrash.addEventListener('click', function(e){
    var photosDir =    Titanium.Filesystem.getFile
      (Titanium.Filesystem.applicationDataDirectory,'photos');

    var fileName = 'photo-' + scrollingView.currentPage.toString()
      + '.png';

    var imageFile = Titanium.Filesystem.getFile
      (photosDir.nativePath, fileName);

    if (imageFile.exists()) {
      //then we can delete it because it exists
      imageFile.deleteFile();
      alert('Your file ' + fileName + ' was deleted!');
    }
  });

win.add(buttonTrash);
```

How it works...

File manipulation is all done using methods on the file object, unlike many other languages where a "delete" function normally means passing the file object into said function to be deleted. In our recipe, you can see we're simply creating the file object as we did previously in the recipe on saving photos to the filesystem. But instead of writing the object to disk, we're checking its existence and then calling `[file-object].deleteFile()`. All file manipulations in Titanium is done in this manner. For example, if you wanted to rename the file, you would simply create the object and call the `rename()` method, passing in the new value as a string parameter.

You may have also noticed that we gave the trash button a parameter called `zIndex`, which we have set to 2. The `zIndex` defines the stack order of a component. Components with a higher `zIndex` will always appear above those with a lower `zIndex`. In this case, we've given the trash button an index of 2, so that it appears above the other elements whose default `zIndex` value is 0.

The following screenshot shows the trash icon visible on our newly saved file, and the message alert that appears confirming it's deletion from the filesystem:

There's more...

A full list of the `Titanium.Filesystem.File` methods is available at the Appcelerator's website under the current API documentation, at: `http://developer.appcelerator.com/apidoc/mobile/latest/Titanium.Filesystem.File-object`

5
Connecting your Apps with Social Media and E-mail

In this chapter, we will cover:

- ► Composing and sending an e-mail
- ► Adding attachments to an e-mail
- ► Setting up a custom Facebook application
- ► Integrating Facebook into your Titanium App
- ► Posting on your Facebook wall
- ► Connecting to Twitter using OAuth
- ► Uploading an image using PHP and HttpRequest
- ► Sending a tweet through Birdhouse and OAuth

Introduction

Once thought to be the domain of the geeky Gen Y, social media has grown exponentially over the past few years into the hottest area of the web. Facebook now has over 500 million users worldwide, twice the population of the United States! Twitter was once the place where you'd hear about what someone had just eaten for breakfast, now it's the first place many people go to for breaking news. The rise of smartphones and mobile applications has hastened the growth of these social networking services as online socializing is no longer confined to a desktop. People can be seen using Facebook and Twitter, among other services, while on the train, in their cars, and pretty much anywhere.

It's because these services are so ubiquitous that many people now expect them to be a standard service from within an application. A simple app, such as one that lists RSS feeds from news sites, is made that much more useful when the user can tweet, post, or e-mail articles at the touch of a button. In this chapter, we will begin with the original social communication medium, e-mail, before continuing to show you how to integrate the world's largest social networking services, Facebook and Twitter, into your application.

Pre-requisites

You should already be familiar with Titanium basics, including creating UI objects and using Titanium Studio. Additionally, to test functionality, you are going to need an account from Twitter and an account from Facebook. You will also need to have an e-mail account set up on your iPhone or Android device.

- ► You can signup for Facebook free of charge at: `http://www.facebook.com`
- ► You can sign up for Twitter free of charge at: `http://twitter.com`
- ► Google provides free e-mail services that are easily set up on both iPhone and Android. You can sign up at: `http://www.google.com/mail`

 Complete source code for this entire chapter can be found in `/Chapter 5/PhotoShare`.

Composing and sending an e-mail

We're going to start this chapter with the simplest form of social communication, both in terms of use and in terms of development—e-mail.

If you are intending to follow the entire chapter and build the PhotoShare app then pay careful attention to the first *Getting ready* section for this recipe, as it will guide you through setting up the project.

Getting ready

To prepare for this recipe, open up Titanium Studio and log in if you have not already done so. If you need to register a new account, you can do so for free directly from within the application. Once you are logged in, click on **New Project**, and the details window for creating a new project will appear. Enter in `PhotoShare` as the name of the app, and fill in the rest of the details with your own information.

 Complete source code for this recipe can be found in the `/Chapter 5/Recipe 1` folder.

How to do it...

Our project has now been created using Titanium Studio. Let's get down to business! Open up the `app.js` file in your editor and remove all existing code. After you have done that, type in the following and then hit save:

```
// this sets the background color of the master UIView (when there are
no windows/tab groups on it)
Titanium.UI.setBackgroundColor('#000');

//this variable will hold our image data blob from the device's
gallery
var selectedImage = null;

var win1 = Titanium.UI.createWindow({
  title:'Tab 1',
  backgroundImage: 'images/background.jpg'
});

var label = Titanium.UI.createLabel({
  width:  280,
  height: 'auto',
  top: 20,
  left: 20,
  color: '#fff',
  font: {fontSize: 18, fontFamily: 'Helvetica', fontWeight:
    'bold'},
  text: 'Photo Share: \nEmail, Facebook & Twitter'
});
win1.add(label);

var imageThumbnail = Titanium.UI.createImageView({
  width: 100,
  height: 120,
  left: 20,
  top: 90,
  backgroundColor: '#000',
  borderSize: 10,
  borderColor: '#fff'
});
win1.add(imageThumbnail);

var buttonSelectImage = Titanium.UI.createButton({
  width:  100,
```

```
    height:  30,
    top: 220,
    left: 20,
    title:  'Choose'
});
buttonSelectImage.addEventListener('click',function(e){
    //obtain an image from the gallery
    Titanium.Media.openPhotoGallery({

        success:function(event)
        {
            selectedImage = event.media;

            // set image view
            Ti.API.debug('Our type was: '+event.mediaType);
            if(event.mediaType == Ti.Media.MEDIA_TYPE_PHOTO)
            {
                imageThumbnail.image = selectedImage;
            }
        },
            cancel:function()
            {
                //user cancelled the action from within
                //the photo gallery
            }
    });
});
win1.add(buttonSelectImage);

var txtTitle = Titanium.UI.createTextField({
    width: 160,
    height: 35,
    left: 140,
    top: 90,
    value: 'Message title...',
    borderStyle: 2,
    backgroundColor: '#fff'
});
win1.add(txtTitle);

var txtMessage = Titanium.UI.createTextArea({
    width: 160,
    height: 120,
    left: 140,
```

```
    top: 130,
    value: 'Message text...',
    font: {fontSize: 15},
    borderStyle: 2,
    backgroundColor: '#fff'
});
win1.add(txtMessage);

win1.open();
```

The previous code lays out our basic application and integrates a simple photo gallery selector, much as we did in the previous chapter (*Chapter 4, Enhancing your Apps with Audio, Video, and the Camera*). We will now create a new button which will call a function to create and display the e-mail dialog when tapped:

```
//create your email
function postToEmail() {
  var emailDialog = Titanium.UI.createEmailDialog();
  emailDialog.subject = txtTitle.value;
  emailDialog.toRecipients = ['info@packtpub.com'];
  emailDialog.messageBody = txtMessage.value;
  emailDialog.open();
}

var buttonEmail = Titanium.UI.createButton({
  width:  280,
  height:  35,
  top: 280,
  left: 20,
  title: 'Send Via Email'
});

buttonEmail.addEventListener('click', function(e){
  if(selectedImage != null) {
    postToEmail();
  } else {
    alert('You must select an image first!');
  }
});

win1.add(buttonEmail);
```

Once you have completed typing in your source code, run your app in the simulator or on your device. You should be able to select an image from the photo gallery, and then type in a title and message for your e-mail using the text fields. This will happen before clicking on the `buttonEmail` object to launch the e-mail dialog window with your message and title attached. Note that if you are using the simulator and you don't have some photos in the gallery already, the best way to obtain some is by visiting `http://images.google.com` in mobile Safari, and searching for images. You can then save them to the photo gallery on the simulator by clicking on and holding the image until the **Save Image** pop-up appears.

How it works...

The first block of code is creating our layout view with a single window and a number of basic components, all of which has already been covered in chapters 1 through 4.

The EmailDialog itself is created using the `Titanium.UI.createEmailDialog()` method and only requires a few simple parameters in order to be able to send a basic e-mail message. The `subject`, `messageBody` and `toRecipients` parameters are standard e-mail fields. While it is not necessary to provide these fields in order to launch an e-mail dialog, you will normally provide at least one or two of these as a matter of course. While the `subject` and `messageBody` fields are both simple strings, it should be noted that the `toRecipients` parameter is actually a basic array. You can add multiple recipients by simply adding another array parameter. For example, if we chose to send our e-mail to two different users, we could write the following:

```
emailDialog.toRecipients = ['info@packtpub.com',
                            'me@boydlee.com'];
```

You can also add BCC or CC recipients in the same manner, using the `ccRecipients` and `bccRecipients` methods of the e-mail dialog respectively. Finally, we launch the e-mail dialog using the `open()` method, at which point you should see something like the following standard e-mail dialog appear in your application:

One more thing

You can use the e-mail dialog's event listener, *complete*, in order to tell when an e-mail has been successfully sent or not. The `result` property in your event handler will provide you with the status of your e-mail, which will be one of the following strings:

- CANCELLED (iOS only)
- FAILED
- SENT
- SAVED (iOS only)

Adding attachments to an e-mail

Now we have a basic e-mail dialog up and running, but ideally what we want to do is attach the photo that we selected from our photo gallery to our new e-mail message. Luckily for us, Titanium makes this easy by exposing a method, `addAttachment()`, that accepts a local path of the file we want to attach.

 Complete source code for this recipe can be found in the `/Chapter 5/Recipe 2` folder.

How to do it...

Adding an attachment is usually as simple as passing the `addAttachment()` method of the e-mail dialog and the location of the file or blob you wish to attach, for example:

```
//add an image from the Resource/images directory
emailDialog.addAttachment('images/my_test_photo.png');
```

Our case is a bit trickier than this though. In order to successfully attach our chosen image, we need to first save it temporarily to the file system, and then pass the file system path to `addAttachment()`. Alter your `postToEmail` function to match the following code:

```
//create your email
function postToEmail() {

  var newDir = Titanium.Filesystem.getFile(
    Titanium.Filesystem.applicationDataDirectory,
  'attachments');

  if(!newDir.exists()) { newDir.createDirectory(); }

  //write out the image file to the attachments directory
  writeFile = Titanium.Filesystem.getFile(newDir.nativePath,
    'temp-image.jpg');

  writeFile.write(selectedImage);
  var emailDialog = Titanium.UI.createEmailDialog();
  emailDialog.subject = txtTitle.value;
  emailDialog.toRecipients = ['info@packtpub.com'];
  emailDialog.messageBody = txtMessage.value;
```

```
    //add an image via attaching the saved file
    emailDialog.addAttachment(writeFile);

    emailDialog.open();
}
```

How it works...

As you can see from the code, an attachment can be added to your e-mail dialog as a blob object, a file, or from a file path. In our example, we are saving the image from our photo gallery to a temporary file first, before adding it to the e-mail dialog, in order to have it displayed as a proper image attachment (as seen in the following screenshot). You can also call the `addAttachment` method multiple times. However, be aware that multiple attachments are currently only supported on the iPhone.

Setting up a custom Facebook application

Integrating Facebook into your Titanium application may seem like a daunting prospect at first. However, once you understand the steps necessary you will see it's not really too hard at all! Before you can allow users to post or retrieve Facebook content from your mobile app, you will first need to set-up an application on Facebook itself. This application will provide you with the necessary API keys you need before the user can authorize your mobile application to post and get content on their behalf.

How to do it...

Firstly, you will need to log in to Facebook using the e-mail address and password you signed up with. If you do not have a Facebook account, you will need to create one for the first time. Don't worry though as it is completely free! You will then need to add the **Developer App** to your Facebook account. You can do this by simply searching for `Developer` in the search bar, and then clicking on through until it is added to your account:

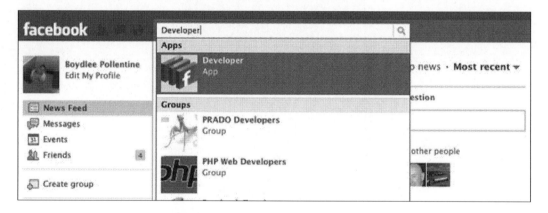

Once you have the Developer application added to your account and loaded, simply click on the **Set Up New App** button on the Developer homepage. The **Create Application** screen will then appear, allowing you to give your application a name and requesting that you agree to Facebook's terms and conditions before proceeding. We have called our app `PhotoShare Titanium`, however, you may use whatever name you wish:

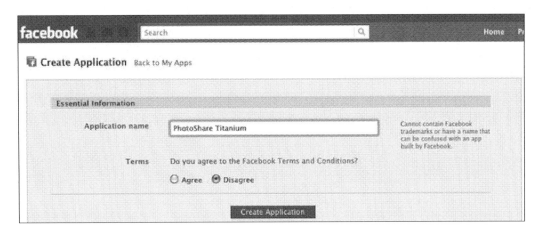

On the next screen that appears, give your application a description and fill in the other requested fields as required. When you have finished, simply save your changes. The final screen in the process provides us with the all important information we need in order to connect our Titanium application to the Facebook API. There are three important values here you are going to need in the next recipe, so be sure to write them down somewhere safe!

These fields are:

- **Application ID**
- **API Key**
- **App Secret**

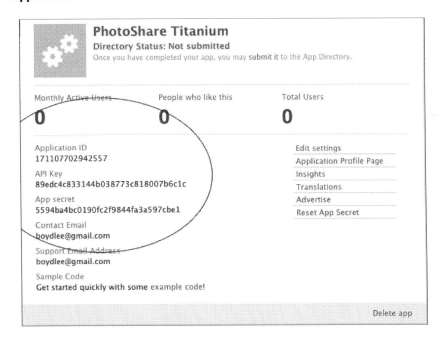

Integrating Facebook into your Titanium App

Now that we have a Facebook application set up, we can get down to connecting our Titanium application to it. Luckily for us, Appcelerator has integrated Facebook's new Graph API tightly into Titanium from version 1.6.0 onwards, so connecting and publishing to the Facebook platform is quite easy!

 Complete source code for this recipe can be found in the `/Chapter 5/Recipe 4` folder.

How to do it...

The first thing we need to do is create a new button which will authorize our Titanium app to publish data on our user's behalf. Enter in the following code in your `app.js` file to create a new button underneath the existing **email user** button:

```
//create your facebook session and post to fb
function postToFacebook() {
   //if the user is not logged in, do so, else post to wall
   if(Titanium.Facebook.loggedIn == false) {
     Titanium.Facebook.appid = '<your app id>';
     Titanium.Facebook.permissions = ['publish_stream'];

     // Permissions your app needs
     Titanium.Facebook.addEventListener('login', function(e)
       {
         if(e.success) {
         alert('You are now logged in!');
       } else if(e.error) {
         alert('Error: ' + e.error);
       } else if(e.cancelled) {
         alert('You cancelled the login');
       }
     });

     //call the facebook authorize method to login
     Titanium.Facebook.authorize();
   }
}

var buttonFacebook = Titanium.UI.createButton({
    width:  280,
    height:  35,
    top: 330,
```

```
        left: 20,
        title: 'Send Via Facebook'
});

buttonFacebook.addEventListener('click', function(e){
    if(selectedImage != null) {
        postToFacebook();
    } else {
        alert('You must select an image first!');
    }
});

    win1.add(buttonFacebook);
```

Now select an image and click on the Facebook button. If you entered in your client ID correctly (which you would have obtained by following the previous recipe) then you should see a login window open up and connect to the Facebook website, showing your application and the permissions it is requesting, as shown in the following example screenshots:

How it works...

We're creating a function that provides Facebook functionality to our application, and allows us to log in to Facebook and let the user accept the permissions we require in order to post to their wall. This function allows us to authenticate against the Facebook API using the App ID that we created in the previous recipe.

This authorization, when successful, allows the user to log in and agree to your request to use certain permissions against their Facebook account. A successful authorization will return and save a Facebook Token. This token is essentially a random string that contains all of the user ID and permission data we will need to execute Facebook Graph requests against the authorized user's account. A successful login will set the `Titanium.Facebook.loggedIn` variable to true, and in the next recipe, we will extend our `postToFacebook` function, using this variable as part of a request to post our chosen photo to our Facebook wall.

Posting on your Facebook wall

Now that we are able to authenticate against Facebook, it's time to post a photo from the gallery to our wall! To achieve this, we need to use Facebook's Graph API, making a call to the correct graph function, with the correct permissions.

[Complete source code for this recipe can be found in the `/Chapter 5/Recipe 5` folder.]

How to do it...

Let's extend our new `postToFacebook()` function by writing a new if-else statement which will take a couple of parameters and execute a Graph request against the Facebook API. Extend the `postToFacebook()` function in `app.js`, so that it matches the following code:

```
//create your facebook session and post to fb
function postToFacebook() {
   //if the user is not logged in, do so, else post to wall
   if(Titanium.Facebook.loggedIn == false) {
     Titanium.Facebook.appid = '252235321506456';
     Titanium.Facebook.permissions = ['publish_stream'];

     // Permissions your app needs
     Titanium.Facebook.addEventListener('login', function(e)
       {
         if(e.success) {
```

```
          alert('You are now logged in!');
        } else if(e.error) {
          alert('Error: ' + e.error);
        } else if(e.cancelled) {
          alert('You cancelled the login');
        }
    });

    //call the facebook authorize method to login
    Titanium.Facebook.authorize();
  }
  else {
    //Now post the photo after you've confirmed
    //that we have an access token
    var data = {
      caption: 'I am posting a photo to my facebook page!',
      picture: selectedImage
    };

    Titanium.Facebook.requestWithGraphPath('me/photos',
      data, "POST", function(e) {

        if (e.success) {
          alert( "Success! Your image has been posted to
            your Facebook wall.");
          Ti.API.info("Success! The image you posted has
            the new ID: " + e.result);
        }
         else {
          alert('Your image could not be posted to Facebook
            at this time. Try again later.');
          Ti.API.error(e.error);
        }
    });

  } //end if else loggedIn
}
```

Now run the application in your emulator or device. If you post an image successfully, you should end up seeing an alert dialog appear in your app, the ID of the new image object from the graph API appear in your developer console, and the photo appear as a post on your Facebook wall!

How it works...

We extended the `postToFacebook()` function that we created in our previous recipe, updating it to first log in to the Facebook API, and then on subsequent post attempts to send a graph request along with a photo to our Facebook Wall.

We can now use Facebook's Graph API (encapsulated in our new `graphRequest` function) to execute our request, passing it the session token we retrieved from the authentication dialog in the previous recipe, along with the name of the graph method we want to call (`me/photos`), and the data properties that method requires. In the case of the `me/photos` method, these two properties are:

- **caption**: A string value which will accompany our image file
- **picture**: A blob/image containing our image data

Using the Graph API and the Facebook login and post function which we have built, it is possible to execute any kind of graph request in your app that Facebook (and your user permissions) will allow. The following screenshot shows an example post:

Connecting to Twitter using OAuth

Appcelerator doesn't currently provide an integrated method of connecting to Twitter in your Titanium applications. However, there are plenty of other options available. One of the best libraries is provided by Joe Purcell and is called "Birdhouse". In this recipe we are going to set up a Twitter application online, get the necessary API keys together (much the same as we did for Facebook), and then implement the OAuth libraries from Google, and finally, the Birdhouse Titanium module.

 Complete source code for this recipe can be found in the /Chapter 5/Recipe 6 folder.

How to do it...

Before we can try to implement the Birdhouse and OAuth libraries, we first need to create an application through Twitter. If you do not have a Twitter account, you will need to create one for the first time. Don't worry though as it is completely free! Log in to your Twitter account at https://dev.twitter.com/apps/new and, once Twitter authenticates your details, you'll be able to create a new Twitter application.

Fill in all of the fields with your own details. For our purposes, we have called the Twitter app `PhotoShare` and set the company and website to that of Packt Publishing. Ensure the application type is set to `Browser`, and that the Default Access Type is set to `Read & Write`. All other fields can either be created as you see fit, or left blank. Enter in the Captcha code and click on **Register Application**, accepting the terms of service as you do.

Once that is done, your application is ready to receive requests from Titanium. Before we can implement the Birdhouse library though, we first need to grab the `oauth.js` and `sha1.js` source files from Google. You can download these from their SVN repository at `http://oauth.googlecode.com/svn/code/javascript/`. Download and save these two files to a new folder called `lib` inside your existing `Resources` folder. Then, navigate your browser to `https://github.com/jpurcell/birdhouse` and download the `birdhouse.js` module file, again saving it to your `Resources` folder.

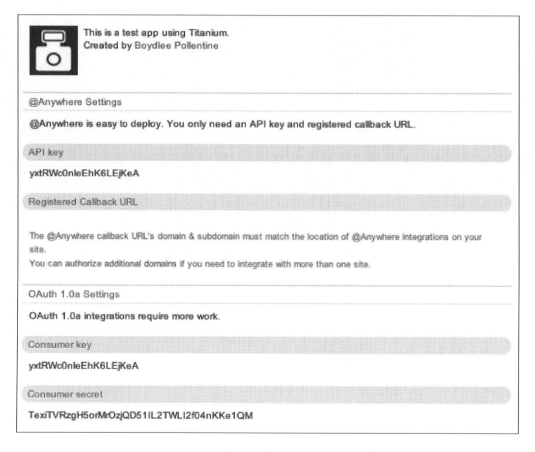

The final step now is including the `birdhouse.js` library into our `app.js` file and executing the Twitter authorization process. First of all, include the library at the top of your `app.js` file:

```
Ti.include('birdhouse.js');
```

We then need to create a new button to authorize and eventually post our Tweet. Enter the following code near the bottom of your `app.js` replacing the `consumer_key` and `consumer_secret` values with the ones provided to you on the Twitter app page:

```
//create your twitter session and post a tweet
function postToTwitter()
{
  var BH = new BirdHouse({
    consumer_key: "your-consumer-key",
    consumer_secret: "your-consumer-secret"
  });

  //call the birdhouse authorize() method
  BH.authorize();
}

var buttonTwitter = Titanium.UI.createButton({
  width:  280,
  height:  35,
  top: 375,
  left: 20,
  title: 'Send Via Twitter'
});
buttonTwitter.addEventListener('click', function(e){
    if(selectedImage != null) {
      postToTwitter();
    } else {
      alert('You must select an image first!');
    }
});
win1.add(buttonTwitter);
```

That's it! You should now be able to choose an image, and then click on the new **Post To Twitter** button at the bottom of the screen. The authorization screen, with our Twitter applications details, should appear and you should be able to log in to Twitter using your existing username and password, as seen in the following screenshot:

Uploading an image using PHP and HttpRequest

There are a number of ways to post an image to Twitter, including using a service such as yfrog or TwitPic. However, for this example we are going to post the image to our own server using PHP and return back the URL. You will need a server running PHP with the GDImage for this recipe to work. There are plenty of cheap or free PHP hosting services online if you don't already have a server. Alternatively, if you are proficient in another web language (such as ASP. NET) you can always rewrite the sample code as you see fit.

Complete source code for this recipe can be found in the
`/Chapter 5/Recipe 7` folder.

How to do it...

Create a new file on your server called `upload.php` and save it with the following contents:

```php
<?php

$target = getcwd();
$target = $target .'/'. $_POST['randomFilename'];

if(move_uploaded_file($_FILES['media']['tmp_name'], $target))
{
  $filename = $target;

  // Get dimensions of the original image
  list($current_width, $current_height) = getimagesize($filename);

  // The x and y coordinates on the original image where we
  // will begin cropping the image
  $left = 0;
  $top = 0;

  // This will be the final size of the image (e.g. how many pixels
    // left and down we will be going)
  $crop_width = $current_width;
  $crop_height = $current_height;

  // Resample the image
  $canvas = imagecreatetruecolor($crop_width, $crop_height);
  $current_image = imagecreatefromjpeg($filename);
  imagecopy($canvas, $current_image, 0, 0, $left, $top,
    $current_width, $current_height);
  imagejpeg($canvas, $filename, 100);

  echo 'http://<mysite.com>/'.$_POST['randomFilename'];
}
else
{
  echo "0";
}
?>
```

Now in the `postToTwitter` function in your existing `app.js` file, we are going to extend the code in order to accommodate posting an image to our server. However, before performing any post image code, we will perform an authorized method call to the Birdhouse API and ensure that the user is currently logged into Twitter. We'll also generate a random 5-letter filename. It's important to keep this nice and short to keep the number of characters we're using to a minimum as Twitter messages have a 140-character limit!

```
function randomString(length,current){
  current = current ? current : '';
  return length ? randomString( --length ,
    "abcdefghiklmnopqrstuvwxyz".charAt
    ( Math.floor( Math.random() * 60 ) ) + current ) : current;
}

//create your twitter session and post a tweet
function postToTwitter()
{
  var BH = new BirdHouse({
    consumer_key: "<your consumer key>",
    consumer_secret: "<your consumer secret>"
  });

  if(!BH.authorized){
    BH.authorize();
  }
  else
  {
    //create the httpRequest
    var xhr = Titanium.Network.createHTTPClient();

    //open the httpRequest
    xhr.open('POST','http://<mysite>.com/upload.php');

    xhr.onload = function(response) {
      //the image upload method has finished
      if(this.responseText != '0')
      {
        var imageURL = this.responseText;
        alert('Your image was uploaded to ' + imageURL);

        //now we have an imageURL we can post a tweet
        //using birdhouse!

      }
      else
      {
        alert('The upload did not work! Check your PHP server
          settings.');
      }
```

```
  };

  // send the data
  var r = randomString(5) + '.jpg';
  xhr.send({'media': selectedImage, 'randomFilename': r});
  }
}
```

How it works...

Here we are utilizing some of our existing knowledge in posting via `HttpRequest` and then extending that knowledge to also send across blob data, using PHP and GDImage. This is then used to write that blob data to an image file on our remote server before returning the new URL. You'll notice that we also extended our `postToTwitter` function to check whether the user is already authorized against Twitter or not before performing this post.

Sending a tweet through Birdhouse and OAuth

For our final recipe, we're going to put everything together and, using a combination of our previous recipe's "image post" functionality and the Birdhouse API, post a tweet containing a message from our app and the image URL that accompanies it.

 Complete source code for this recipe can be found in the `/Chapter 5/Recipe 8` folder.

Complete source code for this entire chapter can be found in the `/Chapter 5/PhotoShare` folder.

How to do it...

Alter the `postToTwitter` function in your existing `app.js` file to match the following code by adding our new `BH.tweet` method call. If you already integrated the photo upload code from the previous recipe, then this source code snippet should appear in the `xhr.onload()` event handler:

```
BH.tweet(txtMessage.value + ' ' + this.responseText,
  function(){
    alertDialog = Ti.UI.createAlertDialog({
      message:'Tweet posted!'
    });

    alertDialog.show();
});
```

Try running your application now in the simulator, and after authorization to Twitter (if necessary) your new tweet should get posted directly from your app! Go to `http://twitter.com/yourusername` to see the tweet posted to your timeline (as seen next). Clicking on the link should then load your uploaded photo!

How it works...

This recipe is very simple, as all of the hard work in connecting to Twitter and uploading an image to our server has been taken care of. Therefore pushing our final message via Birdhouse to the Twitter API is actually very easy. Here we are calling the Birdhouse `tweet()` function, which accepts both a message (as a string) and a second parameter that acts as the event handler for the response from Twitter. You can also use this tweet function outside of posting an image or file to the server. Try posting a simple message tweet without the image and code and you'll see it works just as well!

6
Getting to Grips with Events and Properties

In this chapter, we will cover:

- ▸ Reading and writing app properties
- ▸ Firing and capturing events
- ▸ Passing event data between your app and a WebView using custom events

Introduction

This chapter describes the processes of two fundamentally important, yet deceptively simple, parts of the Titanium framework. In this chapter, we'll explain how to go about creating and reading app properties so that you can store data that is accessible from any part of your application. This is similar to how session data or cookies would work if you were building a web-based app.

We'll also go into further detail on events, including a selection of those fired by the various components in Titanium, and custom events that you can define yourself.

Application properties are used for storing data in key/value pairs. These properties can persist between your app's windows, and even beyond single application sessions, much like a website cookie. You can use any combination of upper case or lower case letters and numbers in a property name, but you should mix them with care as JavaScript is case-sensitive. In this regard, `Myname`, `myname`, and `MYNAME` would be three very different properties!

When should you use app properties?

Application properties should be used when one or more of the following points are true:

- ▸ The data consists of simple key/value pairs
- ▸ The data is related to the application rather than the user
- ▸ The data does not require other data in order to be meaningful or useful
- ▸ There only needs to be one version of the data stored at any one time

For example, storing a string/string key pair of `data_url` and `"http://mywebsite.com/data.xml"` would be a valid way to use app properties. This URL could be re-used throughout all of your application screens/windows and is related to your application, rather than your data.

If your data is complex and needs to be joined, ordered, or queried when retrieving it, then you are better off using a local database built with SQLite. If your data is a file or large blob object, (for example, an image) then this is better stored on the filesystem, in the manner described in our previous recipe.

What object types can be stored as app properties?

There are currently five distinct types of objects that can be stored in the app properties module. These include:

- ▸ Booleans
- ▸ Doubles (float values)
- ▸ Integers
- ▸ Strings
- ▸ Lists (arrays)

In the following recipe, we will create a number of app properties and then read them back, printing them out to the console as we do so.

 Complete source code for this entire chapter can be found in the `/Chapter 6/EventsAndProperties`.

Reading and writing app properties

Whether reading or writing values, all app properties are accessed from the `Titanium.App.Properties` namespace. In this recipe, we are going to create a number of properties, all with different types, on the first tab window of our app. We will then read them and output their values to the console from a button in the second tab window. We'll also show you how to check the existence of a property using the `hasProperty` method.

Complete source code for this recipe can be found in the
`/Chapter 6/Recipe 1` folder.

Getting ready

To prepare for this recipe, open up Titanium Studio and log in if you have not already done so. If you need to register a new account, you can do so for free directly from within the application. Once you are logged in, click on **New Project**, and the details window for creating a new project will appear. Enter in `EventsAndProperties` as the name of the app, and fill in the rest of the details with your own information.

Pay attention to the app identifier, which is written normally in reverse domain notation (that is, *com.packtpub.eventsandproperties*). This identifier cannot be easily changed after the project is created and you will need to match it *exactly* when creating provisioning profiles for distributing your apps later on.

How to do it...

Open up the `app.js` file in your editor and leave the existing code, except for the declaration of the two labels and the lines where those labels are added to your tab Windows. After the declaration of the `win1` object, type in the following code:

```
//
//create a button that will define some app properties
//
var buttonSetProperties = Titanium.UI.createButton({
  title: 'Set Properties!',
  top: 50,
  left: 20,
  width: 280,
  height: 40
});

//create event listener
buttonSetProperties.addEventListener('click',function(e){

  Titanium.App.Properties.setString('myString', 'Hello
    world!');
  Titanium.App.Properties.setBool('myBool', true);
  Titanium.App.Properties.setDouble('myDouble', 345.12);
  Titanium.App.Properties.setInt('myInteger', 11);
```

```
Titanium.App.Properties.setList('myList', ['The first
    value', 'The second value','The third value']);

alert('Your app properties have been set!');

}); //end event listener

win1.add(buttonSetProperties);
```

Now, while still in your `app.js` file, add the following code. It should be placed after the declaration of the `win2` object.

```
//
//create a button that will check for some properties
//
var buttonCheckForProperty = Titanium.UI.createButton({
  title: 'Check Property?',
  top: 50,
  left: 20,
  width: 280,
  height: 40
});

//create event listener
buttonCheckForProperty.addEventListener('click',function(e){
  if(Titanium.App.Properties.hasProperty('myString')){
    Ti.API.info('The myString property exists!');
  }

  if(!Titanium.App.Properties.hasProperty('someOtherString')){
    Ti.API.info('The someOtherString property does not exist.');
  }
}); //end event listener

win2.add(buttonCheckForProperty);

//
//create a button that will read and output some app //properties to
the console
//
var buttonGetProperties = Titanium.UI.createButton({
  title: 'Get Properties!',
  top: 50,
  left: 20,
  width: 280
  height: 40
});
```

```
//create event listener
buttonGetProperties.addEventListener('click',function(e){

    Ti.API.info('myString property = ' +
        Titanium.App.Properties.getString('myString'));

    Ti.API.info('myBool property = ' +
        Titanium.App.Properties.getBool('myBool'));

    Ti.API.info('myDouble property = ' +
        Titanium.App.Properties.getDouble('myDouble'));

    Ti.API.info('myInteger property = ' +
        Titanium.App.Properties.getInt('myInteger'));

    Ti.API.info('myList property = ' +
        Titanium.App.Properties.getList('myList'));

}); //end event listener

win2.add(buttonGetProperties);
```

Now, launch the emulator from Titanium Studio and you should see the standard 2-tab navigation view, with a button in each view. Clicking on the **Set** button on the first tab will set your app properties. After you have done so, you can use the buttons on the second tab view to read back individual properties and check the existence of a property. The results will appear in your Titanium Studio console, similar to the following screenshot:

```
[INFO] Compiling JavaScript...one moment
[INFO] No JavaScript errors detected.
[INFO] One moment, building ...
[INFO] Titanium SDK version: 1.6.1
[INFO] iPhone Device family: iphone
[INFO] iPhone SDK version: 4.3
[INFO] iPhone simulated device: iphone
[INFO] Launching application in Simulator
[INFO] Launched application in Simulator (1.54 seconds)
[INFO] Application started
[INFO] EventsAndProperties/1.0 (1.6.1.2fdc0c5)
[INFO] The myString property exists!
[INFO] The someOtherString property does not exist.
[INFO] myString property = Hello world!
[INFO] myBool property = true
[INFO] myDouble property = 345.12
[INFO] myInteger property = 11
[INFO] myList property = The first value,The second value,The
third value
```

How it works...

In this recipe, we are setting a number of app properties, using our **Set Properties!** button. Each property consists of a key/value pair, and therefore requires a property name (also called the 'key') and a property value. To set a property, we use the `set` method, which looks similar to `Titanium.App.Properties.set<type>(key,value)`. We are then retrieving our app properties by using the `get` method, which looks similar to `Titanium.App.Properties.get<type>(key,value)`.

Application properties are loaded into memory as the app launches, and exist in the global scope of the app until either it is closed, or the property is removed from memory using the `Titanium.App.Properties.remove()` method. While there is a memory overhead in using properties in this manner, it means you can efficiently and quickly access them from any part of your application as they are effectively global in scope.

You can also access the entire list of properties stored at any given time using the `Titanium.App.Properties.listProperties` method.

Firing and capturing events

Much of Titanium is built around the concept of event-driven programming. If you have ever written code in Visual Basic, C#, Java or any number of event-driven, object-orientated languages, this concept will already be familiar to you.

Each time a user interacts with a part of your application's interface, or types something in a `TextField,` an event occurs. The event is simply the action the user took (for example, a tap, a scroll, or a key press on the virtual keyboard) and where it took place (for example, on a button, or in this `TextField`). Additionally, some events can indirectly cause other events to fire. For example, when the user selects a menu item that opens a window, it causes another event—the opening of the window.

There are basically two fundamental types of events in Titanium; those you define yourself (a custom event), and those already defined by the Titanium API (a button click event is a good example).

In the following recipes, we will explore a number of Titanium-defined events before showing you how to create custom events that can pass data between your app and a Webview.

As mentioned in the previous recipe, the user can also indirectly cause events to occur. Buttons, for example, have an event called 'click', which occurs when the user clicks on the button on the screen. The code that handles the response to an event is called an event handler.

There are many events that can occur to each object in your Titanium application. The good news is that you don't need to learn about all of them, and those that are already defined are listed in the Titanium API. You simply need to know how they work and how the event data is accessed so you can find out if the object is able to respond to that event.

In this recipe, we will explore the events that occur from a number of common components, using the OptionDialog as an example, and explain how to access the properties of those events. We'll also explain how to create a function that passes the resulting event back to our executing code.

 Complete source code for this recipe can be found in the /Chapter 6/Recipe 2 folder.

How to do it...

Open up the app.js file in your editor, and below your declaration of the win1 object, type in the following code:

```
//create a button that will launch the optiondialog via
//its click event
var buttonLaunchDialog = Titanium.UI.createButton({
  title: 'Launch OptionDialog',
  top: 110,
  left: 20,
  width: 280,
  height: 40
});

//create the event listener for the button
buttonLaunchDialog.addEventListener('click',function(e){
  Ti.API.info(e.source + ' was tapped, it has a title of: ');
  Ti.API.info(e.source.title);
});

//add the launch dialog button to our window
win1.add(buttonLaunchDialog);
```

Now, after you have created the previous code, we are going to create an OptionDialog with an event listener that uses an external function as its event handler. We'll do this in the event handler function for the buttonLaunchDialog:

```
//create the event listener for the button
buttonLaunchDialog.addEventListener('click',function(e){
  Ti.API.info(e.source + ' was tapped, it has a title of: ');
  Ti.API.info(e.source.title);

  var dialog = Titanium.UI.createOptionDialog({
    options:['More than words can say!',
      'Lots!',
```

```
       'It is okay...',
      'I hate ice cream', 'Cancel'],
      cancel: 4,
      title: 'How much do you like ice cream?'
  });

  //add the event listener for the option dialog
  dialog.addEventListener('click', optionDialogEventHandler);

  //show the option dialog
  dialog.show();
});
```

All that is left to do now is create the final event handler function for our `OptionDialog`. Add the following function to your code before the `buttonLaunchDialog`'s event listener:

```
//this is the event handler function for our option dialog
function optionDialogEventHandler(e) {
  alert(e.source + ' index pressed was ' + e.index);
}
```

Try launching your code now in either the iPhone or Android emulator. As seen in the following example screenshots, you should be able to click on the button and execute the launch of the `OptionDialog` through the button's event handler, which in turn can then show an alert executed via the `optionDialogEventHandler`:

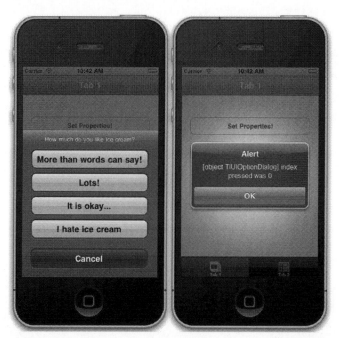

How it works...

First, it's important to reiterate the difference between the event handler and the event listener. The code that listens for a particular event, such as 'click', and then attaches a particular function in response is called the event listener. The code that handles the response to an event is called an event handler. In this recipe, we have shown that event listeners can be launched directly via user interaction, such as a button click, and that event handlers can be executed in one of the following two ways:

▶ Our first method is inline, that is, the event handler function is declared directly within the event listener, such as `buttonLaunchDialog.addEventListener('click', function(e){});`. This is great for quick execution of code that is perhaps used once for a simple task, but does not have a great deal of code reuse.

▶ The second method, and a much more preferable way of using an event handler, is to write it as a separate, self-contained function, such as:

```
function dialogClicked(e) {
   //e.source will tell you what object was clicked
}

//create the event listener for the button
buttonLaunchDialog.addEventListener('click', dialogClicked);
```

This method allows you to get much greater code reuse, and is generally considered a much neater way of organizing your source code.

Passing event data between your app and a Webview using custom events

While we can use the events built into the Titanium API to suit 90 percent of our general purposes, what happens when we want to launch an event that's not covered by one of the standard Titanium components? Luckily for us, Titanium already has this covered with the `fireEvent` method in our `Titanium.App` namespace!

FireEvent allows you to execute an arbitrary event with an event listener name that you determine, and then listen for that event in your code. In this recipe, we are going to get a little bit tricky and write some code that copies an input field's data and displays it on a label back in our app. We will do this by firing off a custom event from within a Webview, which we'll then listen for and respond to back in our Titanium window.

See also

▸ Complete source code for this recipe can be found in the /Chapter 6/Recipe 3 folder.

How to do it...

Open up the app.js file in your editor, and below your declaration of the win2 object, type in the following code to create the Webview:

```
//create a webview and then add that to our
//second window (win2) at the bottom
var webview = Titanium.UI.createWebView({
  url: 'webevent.html',
  width: 320,
  height: 100,
  bottom: 0
});
```

Now, create a new HTML file and call it webevent.html, with the following code. When you have finished, save the HTML file to your project Resources folder.

```
<!DOCTYPE html PUBLIC "-//W3C//DTD HTML 4.01//EN"
  "http://www.w3.org/TR/html4/strict.dtd">
<html lang="en">
<head>
<title>EventHandler Test</title>
</head>
<body>
<input name="myInputField" id="myInputField" value=""
  size="40" />
</body>

<script>
//capture the keypress event in javascript and fire
//an event passing through our textBox's value as a
//property called 'text'
var textBox = document.getElementById("myInputField");
textBox.onkeypress = function () {
  // passing object back with event
  Ti.App.fireEvent('webviewEvent',
  { text: this.value });
};
</script>
</html>
```

All that is left to do now is create the event handler back in our `app.js` file which will copy the input field data from our HTML file as you type in it, and then add our `webview` to the Window. Write the following code below your initial `webview` object declaration in the `app.js` file:

```
//create a label and add to the window
var labelCopiedText = Titanium.UI.createLabel({
  width: 'auto',
  height: 'auto',
  value: '',
  bottom: 120
});
win2.add(labelCopiedText);

//create our custom event listener
Ti.App.addEventListener('webviewEvent', function(e)
  {
    labelCopiedText.text = e.text;
});
win2.add(webview);
```

Run your app in the emulator now and you should be able type in the input field that is within our Webview to see the results mirrored on the label that we positioned above it! You should be able to see a screen just like the one pictured here:

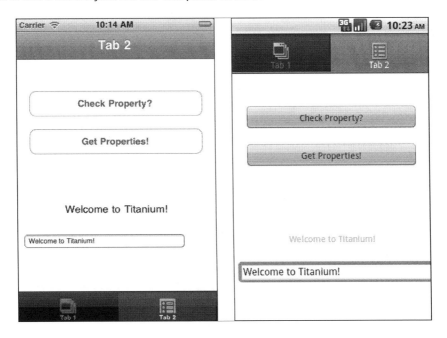

How it works...

Basically, our event fired from the `Titanium.App.fireEvent` method creates a cross-context application event that any JavaScript file can listen to. However, there are two caveats to this. First, the event can only be handled if the same event name is used in both your `fireEvent` call and your listener. As with app properties, this event name is case-sensitive so make sure it is spelled exactly the same way throughout all parts of your application code.

Second, you must pass an object back even if it is empty, and that object must be in a JSON serialized format. This standardization ensures that your data payload is always transportable between contexts.

There's more...

It's also possible to remove an event listener from your code should you no longer need it. You can do this by calling `Titanium.App.removeEventListener` and passing it the name of your event. Note that it is still case-sensitive, so your event name must match exactly! An example for our application of removing the `webviewEvent` would be:

```
Titanium.App.removeEventListener('webviewEvent');
```

7
Creating Animations, Transformations, and Understanding Drag-and-drop

In this chapter, we will cover:

▶ Animating a View using the "animate" method

▶ Animating a View using 2D matrix and 3D matrix transforms

▶ Dragging an ImageView using touch events

▶ Scaling an ImageView using a Slider control

▶ Saving our "Funny Face" image using the toImage() method

Introduction

Almost any control or element in Titanium can have an animation or transform applied to it. This allows you to enhance your applications by adding a level of interactivity and "bling" that your apps would otherwise perhaps not have.

In this chapter, we are going to create a small application that allows the user to choose a "funny face" image, which we are going to position over the top of a photograph of ourselves. We'll use transitions and animations in order to display the funny face pictures and allow the user to adjust the size of his/her photograph and its position so that it fits neatly within the funny-face cutout section.

Finally, we'll combine both our "me" photograph and the funny face into one complete image using the Windows `toImage()` method, letting the user e-mail the resulting image to his/her friends!

 Complete source code for this entire chapter can be found in the `Chapter 7/FunnyFaces` folder.

Animating a View using the "animate" method

Any Window, View, or Component in Titanium can be animated using the `animate` method. This allows you to quickly and confidently create animated objects that can give your applications the "wow" factor. Additionally, you can use animations as a way of holding information or elements off screen until they are actually required. A good example of this would be if you had three different TableViews but only wanted one of those views visible at any one time. Using animations, you could slide those tables in and out of the screen space whenever it suited you, without the complication of creating additional Windows.

In the following recipe, we will create the basic structure of our application by laying out a number of different components and then get down to animating four different ImageViews. These will each contain a different image to use as our "Funny Face" character.

 Complete source code for this recipe can be found in the `/Chapter 7/Recipe 1` folder.

Getting ready

To prepare for this recipe, open up Titanium Studio and log in if you have not already done so. If you need to register a new account, you can do so for free directly from within the application. Once you are logged in, click on **New Project**, and the details window for creating a new project will appear. Enter in `FunnyFaces` as the name of the app, and fill in the rest of the details with your own information.

Pay attention to the app identifier, which is written normally in reverse domain notation (that is, *com.packtpub.funnyfaces*). This identifier cannot be easily changed after the project is created and you will need to match it *exactly* when creating provisioning profiles for distributing your apps later on.

The first thing to do is copy all of the required images into an `images` folder under your project's `Resources` folder. Then, open the `app.js` file in your IDE and replace its contents with the following code. This code will form the basis of our FunnyFaces application layout.

```
// this sets the background color of the master UIView Titanium.
UI.setBackgroundColor('#fff');

//
//create root window
//
var win1 = Titanium.UI.createWindow({
  title:'Funny Faces',
  backgroundColor:'#fff'
});

//this will determine whether we load the 4 funny face
//images or whether one is selected already
var imageSelected = false;

//the 4 image face objects, yet to be instantiated
var image1;
var image2;
var image3;
var image4;

var imageViewMe = Titanium.UI.createImageView({
  image: 'images/me.png',
  width: 320,
  height: 480,
  zIndex: 0
  left: 0,
  top: 0,
  zIndex: 0,
  visible: false
});
win1.add(imageViewMe);

var imageViewFace = Titanium.UI.createImageView({
  image: 'images/choose.png',
  width: 320,
  height: 480,
  zIndex: 1
});
imageViewFace.addEventListener('click', function(e){
  if(imageSelected == false){
```

```
        //transform our 4 image views onto screen so
        //the user can choose one!


    }
});
win1.add(imageViewFace);



//this footer will hold our save button and zoom slider objects
var footer = Titanium.UI.createView({
    height: 40,
    backgroundColor: '#000',
    bottom: 0,
    left: 0,
    zIndex: 2
});
var btnSave = Titanium.UI.createButton({
    title: 'Save Photo',
    width: 100,
    left: 10,
    height: 34,
    top: 3
});
footer.add(btnSave);

var zoomSlider = Titanium.UI.createSlider({
    left: 125,
    top: 8,
    height: 30,
    width: 180
});
footer.add(zoomSlider);

win1.add(footer);

//open root window
win1.open();
```

Build and run your application in the emulator for the first time, and you should end up with a screen that looks just similar to the following example:

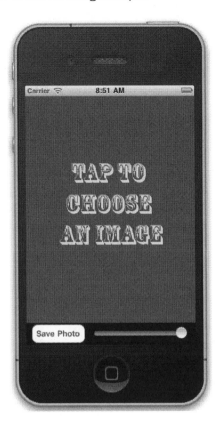

How to do it...

Now, back in the `app.js` file, we are going to animate the four ImageViews which will each provide an option for our funny face image. Inside the declaration of the `imageViewFace` object's event handler, type in the following code:

```
imageViewFace.addEventListener('click', function(e){
  if(imageSelected == false){
    //transform our 4 image views onto screen so
    //the user can choose one!
    image1 = Titanium.UI.createImageView({
      backgroundImage: 'images/clown.png',
      left: -160,
      top: -140,
      width: 160,
      height: 220,
```

```
      zIndex: 2
  });
  image1.addEventListener('click', setChosenImage);
  win1.add(image1);

  image2 = Titanium.UI.createImageView({
    backgroundImage: 'images/policewoman.png',
    left: 321,
    top: -140,
    width: 160,
    height: 220,
    zIndex: 2
  });
  image2.addEventListener('click', setChosenImage);
  win1.add(image2);

  image3 = Titanium.UI.createImageView({
    backgroundImage: 'images/vampire.png',
    left: -160,
    bottom: -220,
    width: 160,
    height: 220,
    zIndex: 2
  });
  image3.addEventListener('click', setChosenImage);
  win1.add(image3);

  image4 = Titanium.UI.createImageView({
    backgroundImage: 'images/monk.png',
    left: 321,
    bottom: -220,
    width: 160,
    height: 220,
    zIndex: 2
  });
  image4.addEventListener('click', setChosenImage);
  win1.add(image4);

  image1.animate({
    left: 0,
    top: 0,
    duration: 500,
    curve: Titanium.UI.ANIMATION_CURVE_EASE_IN
  });
  image2.animate({
    left: 160,
    top: 0,
    duration: 500,
    curve: Titanium.UI.ANIMATION_CURVE_EASE_OUT
  });
```

```
    image3.animate({
      left: 0,
      bottom: 20,
      duration: 500,
      curve: Titanium.UI.ANIMATION_CURVE_EASE_IN_OUT
    });

    image4.animate({
      left: 160,
      bottom: 20,
      duration: 500,
      curve: Titanium.UI.ANIMATION_CURVE_LINEAR
    });
  }
});
```

Now launch the emulator from Titanium Studio and you should see the initial layout with our "Tap To Choose An Image" view visible. Tapping the choose ImageView should now animate our four funny face options onto the screen, as seen in the following screenshot:

How it works...

The first block of code creates the basic layout for our application, which consists of a couple of ImageViews, a footer view holding our "save" button, and the Slider control, which we'll use later on to increase the zoom scale of our own photograph. Our second block of code is where it gets interesting. Here, we're doing a simple check that the user hasn't already selected an image using the `imageSelected` Boolean, before getting into our animated ImageViews, named `image1`, `image2`, `image3`, and `image4`.

The concept behind the animation of these four ImageViews is pretty simple. All we're essentially doing is changing the properties of our control over a period of time, defined by us in milliseconds. Here, we are changing the `top` and `left` properties of all of our images over a period of half a second so that we get an effect of them sliding into place on our screen. You can further enhance these animations by adding more properties to animate, for example, if we wanted to change the opacity of image1 from 50 percent to 100 percent as it slides into place, we could change the code to look something similar to the following:

```
image1 = Titanium.UI.createImageView({
  backgroundImage: 'images/clown.png',
  left: -160,
  top: -140,
  width: 160,
  height: 220,
  zIndex: 2,
  opacity: 0.5
});
image1.addEventListener('click', setChosenImage);
win1.add(image1);

image1.animate({
  left: 0,
  top: 0,
  duration: 500,
  curve: Titanium.UI.ANIMATION_CURVE_EASE_IN,
  opacity: 1.0
});
```

Finally, the curve property of `animate()` allows you to adjust the easing of your animated component. Here, we used all four animation-curve constants on each of our ImageViews. They are:

- `Titanium.UI.ANIMATION_CURVE_EASE_IN`: Accelerate the animation slowly
- `Titanium.UI.ANIMATION_CURVE_EASE_OUT`: Decelerate the animation slowly

- ▶ `Titanium.UI.ANIMATION_CURVE_EASE_IN_OUT`: Accelerate and decelerate the animation slowly

- ▶ `Titanium.UI.ANIMATION_CURVE_LINEAR`: Make the animation speed constant throughout the animation cycles

Animating a View using 2D matrix and 3D matrix transforms

You may have noticed that each of our ImageViews in the previous recipe had a `click` event listener attached to them, calling an event handler named `setChosenImage`. This event handler is going to handle setting our chosen "funny face" image to the `imageViewFace` control. It will then animate all four "funny face" ImageView objects on our screen area using a number of different 2D and 3D matrix transforms.

 Complete source code for this recipe can be found in the `/Chapter 7/Recipe 2` folder.

How to do it...

Replace the existing `setChosenImage` function, which currently stands empty, with the following source code:

```
//this function sets the chosen image and removes the 4
//funny faces from the screen
function setChosenImage(e){
  imageViewFace.image = e.source.backgroundImage;
  imageViewMe.visible = true;

  //create the first transform
  var transform1 = Titanium.UI.create2DMatrix();
  transform1 = transform1.rotate(-180);

  var animation1 = Titanium.UI.createAnimation({
    transform: transform1,
    duration: 500,
    curve: Titanium.UI.ANIMATION_CURVE_EASE_IN_OUT
  });
  image1.animate(animation1);
  animation1.addEventListener('complete',function(e){
    //remove our image selection from win1
    win1.remove(image1);
  });
```

```
//create the second transform
var transform2 = Titanium.UI.create2DMatrix();
transform2 = transform2.scale(0);

var animation2 = Titanium.UI.createAnimation({
  transform: transform2,
  duration: 500,
  curve: Titanium.UI.ANIMATION_CURVE_EASE_IN_OUT
});
image2.animate(animation2);
animation2.addEventListener('complete',function(e){
  //remove our image selection from win1
  win1.remove(image2);
});

//create the third transform
var transform3 = Titanium.UI.create2DMatrix();
transform3 = transform3.rotate(180);
transform3 = transform3.scale(0);

var animation3 = Titanium.UI.createAnimation({
  transform: transform3,
  duration: 1000,
  curve: Titanium.UI.ANIMATION_CURVE_EASE_IN_OUT
});
image3.animate(animation3);
animation3.addEventListener('complete',function(e){
  //remove our image selection from win1
  win1.remove(image3);
});

//create the fourth and final transform
var transform4 = Titanium.UI.create3DMatrix();
transform4 = transform4.rotate(200,0,1,1);
transform4 = transform4.scale(2);
transform4 = transform4.translate(20,50,170);
//the m34 property controls the perspective of the 3D view
transform4.m34 = 1.0/-3000; //m34 is the position at [3,4]
                            //in the matrix

var animation4 = Titanium.UI.createAnimation({
  transform: transform4,
  duration: 1500,
```

```
      curve: Titanium.UI.ANIMATION_CURVE_EASE_IN_OUT
   });
   image4.animate(animation4);
   animation4.addEventListener('complete',function(e){
      //remove our image selection from win1
      win1.remove(image4);
   });

   //change the status of the imageSelected variable
   imageSelected = true;
}
```

How it works...

Again, we are creating animations for each of the four ImageViews, but this time in a slightly different way. Instead of using the built-in `animate` method, we are creating a separate animation object for each ImageView, before calling the ImageView's `animate` method and passing this animation object to it. This method of creating animations allows you to have finer control over them, including the use of transforms.

Transforms have a couple of shortcuts to help you perform some of the most common animation types quickly and easily. The `image1` and `image2` transforms, as shown in the previous code, use the `rotate` and `scale` methods respectively. Scale and rotate in this case are 2D matrix transforms, meaning they only transform the object in two-dimensional space along its X-axis and Y-axis. Each of these transformation types takes a single integer parameter; for scale, it is 0-100 percent and for rotate, the number of it is 0-360 degrees.

Another advantage of using transforms for your animations is that you can easily chain them together to perform a more complex animation style. In the previous code, you can see that both a `scale` and a `rotate` transform are transforming the `image3` component. When you run the application in the emulator or on your device, you should notice that both of these transform animations are applied to the `image3` control!

Finally, the `image4` control also has a transform animation applied to it, but this time we are using a 3D matrix transform instead of the 2D matrix transforms used for the other three ImageViews. These work the same way as regular 2D matrix transforms, except that you can also animate your control in 3D space, along the Z-axis.

It's important to note that animations have two event listeners: `start` and `complete`. These event handlers allow you to perform actions based on the beginning or ending of your animation's life cycle. As an example, you could chain animations together by using the `complete` event to add a new animation or transform to an object after the previous animation has finished. In our previous example, we are using this `complete` event to remove our ImageView from the Window once its animation has finished.

Dragging an ImageView using touch events

Now that we have allowed the user to select a funny face image from our four animated ImageView controls, we need to allow them to adjust the position of their own photo so it fits within the transparent hole that makes up the face portion of our funny face. We are going to do this using the touch events provided by the ImageView control.

 Complete source code for this recipe can be found in the `/Chapter 7/Recipe 3` folder.

How to do it...

The simplest way to perform this task is by capturing the X and Y touch points and moving the ImageView to that location. The code for this is simple. Just add the following code after your declaration of the `imageViewFace` control, but before you add this control to your window:

```
imageViewFace.addEventListener('touchmove', function(e){
  imageViewMe.left = e.x;
  imageViewMe.top = e.y;
});
```

Now, run your app in the emulator, and after selecting a funny face image, attempt to touch-and-drag your photograph around the screen. You should notice that it works but it doesn't seem quite right, does it? This is because we are moving the image based on the top corner position, instead of the center of the object. Let's change our code to instead work on the center point of the `imageViewMe` control, by replacing the previous code with the following source code:

```
imageViewFace.addEventListener('touchstart', function (e) {
  imageViewMe.ox = e.x - imageViewMe.center.x;
  imageViewMe.oy = e.y - imageViewMe.center.y;
});

imageViewFace.addEventListener('touchmove', function(e){
  imageViewMe.center = {
    x:(e.x - imageViewMe.ox),
    y:(e.y - imageViewMe.oy)
  };
});
```

Run your app in the emulator again and after selecting a funny face image, attempt to touch-and-drag your photograph around the screen. This time you should notice a much smoother, more natural feeling drag-and-drop effect! Try positioning your "me" photograph into the center of one of your funny faces, and you should be able to replicate the following screenshot:

How it works...

Here we are using two separate touch events to transform the left and top positioning properties of our `imageViewMe` control. First, we need to find the center point. We do this in our `touchstart` event by the `center.x` and `center.y` properties of our ImageView control and then assign these to a couple of custom variables we have named "ox" and "oy". Doing this within the `touchstart` event ensures that these variables are immediately available to us when the `touchmove` event occurs. Then, within our `touchmove` event, instead of changing the top and left properties of `imageViewMe`, we pass its center property to our new x and y co-ordinates based on the touch events x and y properties, minus the center point we saved as our object's ox and oy variables. This ensures that the movement of the image is nice and smooth!

Scaling an ImageView using a Slider control

We have now created a code to select an animated funny face and we have the ability to move our image around using the drag-and-drop method. We need to be able to scale our "me" photograph using a Slider control and a new transformation.

In the following recipe, we will hook up the event listener of our Slider control and use another 2D matrix transformation, and this time change the scale of our `imageViewMe` control based on the user input.

 Complete source code for this recipe can be found in the /Chapter 7/Recipe 4 folder.

How to do it...

Near the bottom of your current source code, you should have instantiated a Slider control named "`zoomSlider`". We are going to replace that code with a slightly updated version, and then capture the slider's change event in order to scale our `imageViewMe` component based on the value selected. Replace your declaration of the `zoomSlider` component with the following code:

```
var zoomSlider = Titanium.UI.createSlider({
  left: 125,
  top: 8,
  height: 30,
  width: 180,
  minValue: 1,
  maxValue: 100,
  value: 50
});

//create the sliders event listener/handler
zoomSlider.addEventListener('change', function(e){
  //create the scaling transform
  var transform = Titanium.UI.create2DMatrix();
  transform = transform.scale(zoomSlider.value);
  var animation = Titanium.UI.createAnimation({
    transform: transform,
    duration: 100,
    curve: Titanium.UI.ANIMATION_CURVE_EASE_IN_OUT
  });
  imageViewMe.animate(animation);
```

```
});

//finally, add our slider to the footer view
footer.add(zoomSlider);
```

Try running your application in the emulator now, and after selecting a funny face image, you should be able to scale the "me" photograph using the Slider control. Try using it in conjunction with the touch-and-drag from the previous recipe to fit your face inside the funny picture hole, as seen in the following screenshot:

How it works...

We are performing a very similar action to what we did in the second recipe of this chapter. Within the change event handler of our Slider control, we are applying a 2D matrix transform to the `imageViewMe` control, using the scale method. Our slider has been given a minimum value of 0 and a maximum of 100. These values are the relative percentages that we are going to scale our image by. By using a very short duration (for example, 100 milliseconds) on our animation, we can make the movement of the slider almost instantaneously relate to the scale of the "me" photograph.

Saving our "Funny Face" image using the toImage() method

For the very last part of this application, we want to combine the two images together (our "me" photograph and the funny face image we have chosen) and save them to the filesystem as one complete image. To do this, we will hook up the event listener of our save button control and use another common method found on almost all views and control types; `toImage`. Once we've combined our two images together and saved it off to the local filesystem, we'll then create a quick e-mail dialog and attach our funny face to it, allowing the user to send the complete image to his/her friends.

 Complete source code for this recipe can be found in the `/Chapter 7/Recipe 5` folder.

How to do it...

Underneath the instantiation of your `btnSave` object, add the following event listener and handler code:

```
btnSave.addEventListener("click", function(e){
  //hide the footer
  footer.visible = false;

  //do a slight delay before capturing the image
  //so we are certain the footer is hidden!
  setTimeout(function(e){
    //get the merged blob -- note on android you
    //might want to use toBlob() instead of toImage()
    var mergedImage = win1.toImage();

    writeFile = Titanium.Filesystem.getFile(
      Titanium.Filesystem.applicationDataDirectory,
      'funnyface.jpg');
    writeFile.write(mergedImage);

    //now email our merged image file!
    var emailDialog = Titanium.UI.createEmailDialog();
    emailDialog.setSubject("Check out funny face!");
    emailDialog.addAttachment(writeFile);
```

```
emailDialog.addEventListener('complete',function(e) {
  //reset variables so we can do another funny face
  footer.visible = true;
  imageViewFace.image = 'images/choose.png';
  imageSelected = false;
});

emailDialog.open();

}, 250);
});
```

Now, launch your application in the emulator or on your device, again going through all of the steps until you have chosen a funny face, and adjust the layout of your photograph accordingly. When done, hit the **save** button and you should see an e-mail dialog appear with your combined image visible as an attachment.

How it works...

The `toImage` method simply takes a combined screenshot of the element in question. In our case, we are performing the command on `win1`, our root `Window` object. To do this, we are simply hiding our footer control and then setting a short timeout. When elapsed, it uses `toImage` to take a combined screenshot of both our `imageViewMe` and `imageViewFace` controls, which we then save to the filesystem.

There is another method that most controls have called `toBlob`, which works in a very similar manner to `toImage`. Depending on what you are trying to achieve, you can generally use either one of these methods. However, at times, you will find that the Titanium API will contain bugs and only one of them may work. In particular, the `toBlob` method works far better on Android devices than the `toImage` method does. However, as the Titanium platform grows more stable, you can expect better performance from both of these API calls. Additionally, you would use the `toBlob` method in order to store blob data in a local database using SQLite, though in general this approach is not normally used as it is very memory intensive. Saving blob objects to the filesystem is the recommended approach.

The following screenshot shows our final combined image, which has been saved to the filesystem and attached to a new e-mail dialog ready to be shared among the user's friends and family!

8
Interacting with Native Phone Applications and APIs

In this chapter, we will cover:

▶ Creating an Android Options menu

▶ Accessing the contacts address book

▶ Storing and retrieving data via the clipboard

▶ Creating a background service on the iPhone

▶ Displaying local notifications on the iPhone

▶ Displaying Android notifications using intents

▶ Storing your Android app on the device's SD-card

Introduction

While Titanium allows you to create native apps that are almost totally cross-platform, it is inevitable that some devices will inherently have operating system and hardware differences that are specific to them (particularly between Android and iOS). For example, anyone who has used both Android and iPhone devices would immediately recognize the very different way the notification systems are set up. However, there are other platform-specific limitations that are very specific to the Titanium API.

In this chapter, we'll show you how to create and use some of these device-specific components and APIs in your applications. Unlike most chapters in this book, this one does not follow a singular, coherent application. So feel free to read each recipe in whichever order you wish.

Creating an Android Options menu

Option menus are an important part of the Android user interface. They are the primary collection of menu items for a screen and appear when the user presses the **MENU** button on their device. In this recipe we are going to create an Android Options Menu and add it to our screen, giving each option its own click event with an action.

Getting ready

To prepare for this recipe, and all recipes in this chapter, open up Titanium Studio and log in if you have not already done so. You can either use the same application for each of the recipes in this chapter or create a new one, the choice is up to you.

The icons and code for this application is available in the Chapter 8/Recipe 1 folder.

Complete source code for this recipe can be found in the /Chapter 8/Recipe 1 folder.

How to do it...

Open up the app.js file in your IDE and enter in the following code:

```
//create the root window
var win1 = Titanium.UI.createWindow({
  title: 'Android Options Menu',
  backgroundColor: '#ccc'
});

if(Titanium.Platform.osname == 'android')
{
  //references the current android activity
  var activity = Ti.Android.currentActivity;

  //create our menu
  activity.onCreateOptionsMenu = function(e) {
    var menu = e.menu;

    //menu button 1
    var menuItem1 = menu.add({ title: "Item 1" });
    menuItem1.setIcon("item1.png");
    menuItem1.addEventListener("click", function(e) {
      alert("Menu item #1 was clicked");
    });
```

```
    //menu button 2
    var menuItem2 = menu.add({
      title: "Show Item #4",
      itemId: 2
    });
    menuItem2.setIcon("item2.png");
    menuItem2.addEventListener("click", function(e) {
      menu.findItem(4).setVisible(true);
    });

    //menu button 3
    var menuItem3 = menu.add({ title: "Item 3" });
    menuItem3.setIcon("item3.png");
    menuItem3.addEventListener("click", function(e) {
      alert("Menu item #3 was clicked");
    });

    //menu button 4 (will be hidden)
    var menuItem4 = menu.add({
      title: "Hide Item #4",
      itemId: 4
    });
    menuItem4.setIcon("item4.png");
    menuItem4.addEventListener("click", function(e) {
      menu.findItem(4).setVisible(false);
    });

  };

  //turn off the item #4 by default
  activity.onPrepareOptionsMenu = function(e) {
    var menu = e.menu;
   menu.findItem(4).setVisible(false);
  };
}

win1.open();
```

Build and run your application in the Android emulator for the first time. When you press the "menu" button on your device/emulator you should end up seeing a screen that looks just like the following example. Tapping on the first menu item should execute its click event and show you an alert dialog. An example of this can be seen in the following screenshot:

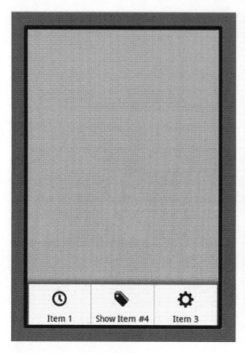

How it works...

First, it is important to note that the code in this recipe is applicable to Android only. The iOS platform doesn't have a physical menu button like an Android device, and therefore doesn't have an Option menu. On Android, these menus help to facilitate user actions. We can see this occurring in the `click` event of the first menu item, where we are using an event handler to capture this event and show a simple alert dialog.

The fourth option in the menu is altered by utilizing the "`onPrepareOptionsMenu`" event, which is executed prior to the menu being added to the screen. You can enable, disable, add, or remove items within this event handler. In this recipe, we are hiding the fourth menu option by setting its `visible` state to *false*, which we can change again to *true* within the event handler of the second menu option.

Menu icon sizes for Android devices

Your menu icons should be flat, pictured "face on", and greyscale. According to the Android guidelines, all menu icons should use the same color palette and effects in order to maintain consistency. Icon sizes for each of the Android screen density sizes are listed below.

- ▸ Menu icon dimensions for high-density (hdpi) screens:
  - ❑ Full Asset: 72 x 72 px
  - ❑ Icon: 48 x 48 px
  - ❑ Square Icon: 44 x 44 px

- ▸ Menu icon dimensions for medium-density (mdpi) screens:
  - ❑ Full Asset: 48 x 48 px
  - ❑ Icon: 32 x 32 px
  - ❑ Square Icon: 30 x 30 px

- ▸ Menu icon dimensions for low-density (ldpi) screens:
  - ❑ Full Asset: 36 x 36 px
  - ❑ Icon: 24 x 24 px
  - ❑ Square Icon: 22 x 22

Accessing the contacts address book

There will be times when you want the user to access existing data from their device in order to populate some fields or a database within your own application. Possibly, the best example of this is the utilization of the address book and contact details. For example, if you built an application that primarily was meant for sharing data over e-mail, using the contact address book on the device would allow the user to select contacts they already have from a selection list (as opposed to having to remember or re-enter the data separately).

In this recipe, we'll create a basic interface that accesses our address book and pulls back a contact's details, filling in our interface components including some text fields and an image view as we do so. Before you start, make sure your device or emulator has some contacts available in it by choosing the *Contacts* icon on iPhone or the *People* icon on Android and adding at least one entry.

 Complete source code for this recipe can be found in the /Chapter 8/Recipe 2 folder.

How to do it...

Open up the `app.js` file in your IDE and enter in the following code:

```
//create the root window
var win1 = Titanium.UI.createWindow({
  title: 'Android Options Menu',
  backgroundColor: '#ccc'
});


//add the textfields
var txtName = Titanium.UI.createTextField({
  width: 280,
  top: 150,
  left: 20,
  height: 40,
  backgroundColor: '#fff',
  borderRadius: 3,
  hintText: 'Friend\'s name...',
  paddingLeft: 3
});
win1.add(txtName);

var txtEmail = Titanium.UI.createTextField({
  width: 280,
  top: 200,
  left: 20,
  height: 40,
  backgroundColor: '#fff',
  borderRadius: 3,
  hintText: 'Contact\'s email address...',
  paddingLeft: 3,
  keyboardType: Titanium.UI.KEYBOARD_EMAIL
});
win1.add(txtEmail);

//this is the user image
var imgView = Titanium.UI.createImageView({
  width: 80,
  left: 20,
  height: 80,
  top: 45,
  image: 'no_avatar.gif'
```

```
});
win1.add(imgView);

var contactButton = Titanium.UI.createButton({
  title: 'Select a contact...',
  left: 20,
  top: 10,
  height: 28,
  width: 280
});
contactButton.addEventListener('click', function(e){
  //
  //if array of details is specified, the detail view will be
  //shown
  //when the contact is selected.  this will also trigger
  //e.key, and e.index in the success callback
  //
  Titanium.Contacts.showContacts({
    selectedProperty: function(e) {
      Ti.API.info(e.type + ' - '+ e.value);
      txtEmail.value = e.email;
    },
    selectedPerson: function(e) {
      var person = e.person;
      txtEmail.value = person.email.home[0];
      if (person.image != null) {
        imgView.image = person.image;
      }
      else {
        imgView.image = 'no_avatar.gif';
        avatar = 'no_avatar.gif';
      }

      txtName.value = person.firstName + ' ' + person.lastName;
    }
  });
});

win1.add(contactButton);

win1.open();
```

How it works...

Access to the address book differs depending on the platform. On the Android operating system you will have read-only access to the contacts list, whereas on the iPhone you will have full read/write privileges. Therefore, it pays to keep in mind that methods such as `createPerson` will not be available for use on Android devices.

All access to the device's contacts are available through the `Titanium.Contacts` namespace. In this recipe, we built a basic screen with some text fields and an image view, which we're populating by loading up the contacts API and choosing an entry from the device's contact list. To do this, we are executing the `showContacts()` method, which has two distinct callback functions:

1. `SelectedProperty`: This callback is executed when the user chooses a person's property, rather than a singular contact entry

2. `SelectedPerson`: This call-back is executed when the user chooses a person's entry

In our example recipe, we are utilizing the `SelectedPerson` function and assigning the callback property `(e)` to a new object named `person`. From here we can access the `field` properties of the contact that were chosen from the device's contact list, such as phone, e-mail, name, and contact photograph, and then assign these variables to the relevant fields in our own application. The following screenshots show the contact's screen both empty and filled out after choosing a contact from the device's list:

Storing and retrieving data via the clipboard

The clipboard is used to store textual and object data so it can be utilized between different screens and applications on your device. While both iOS and Android have built-in clipboard capability, Titanium extends this by letting you programmatically access and write data to the clipboard. In this recipe, we will create a screen with two text fields and a series of buttons that allow us to programmatically copy data from one text field and paste it into another.

 Complete source code for this recipe can be found in the /Chapter 8/Recipe 3 folder.

How to do it...

Open your project's app.js file in your IDE and enter in the following code (deleting any existing code). When finished, run your application in the emulator to test it.

```
var win1 = Titanium.UI.createWindow({
  backgroundColor: '#fff',
  title: 'Copy and Paste'
});

var txtData1 = Titanium.UI.createTextField({
  left: 20,
  width: 280,
  height: 40,
  top: 10,
  borderStyle:Titanium.UI.INPUT_BORDERSTYLE_ROUNDED
});

var txtData2 = Titanium.UI.createTextField({
  left: 20,
  width: 280,
  height: 40,
  top: 60,
  borderStyle:Titanium.UI.INPUT_BORDERSTYLE_ROUNDED
});

var copyButton = Titanium.UI.createButton({
  title: 'Copy',
  width: 80,
  height: 30,
```

```
    left: 20,
    top: 140
});

var pasteButton = Titanium.UI.createButton({
    title: 'Paste',
    width: 80,
    height: 30,
    left: 120,
    top: 140,
    visible: false
});

var clearButton = Titanium.UI.createButton({
    title: 'Clear',
    width: 80,
    height: 30,
    right: 20,
    top: 140
});

function copyTextToClipboard() {
    Ti.UI.Clipboard.setText(txtData1.value);
    copyButton.visible = false;
    pasteButton.visible = true;
}

function pasteTextFromClipboard() {
    txtData2.value = Ti.UI.Clipboard.getText();
    txtData1.value = '';
    copyButton.visible = true;
    pasteButton.visible = false;
}

function clearTextFromClipboard() {
    Ti.UI.Clipboard.clearText();
}

copyButton.addEventListener('click', copyTextToClipboard);
pasteButton.addEventListener('click', pasteTextFromClipboard);
clearButton.addEventListener('click', clearTextFromClipboard);

win1.add(txtData1);
win1.add(txtData2);
win1.add(copyButton);
win1.add(pasteButton);
win1.add(clearButton);
win1.open();
```

How it works...

In this recipe we are copying simple strings to and from the clipboard. However, it is important to note that you can also copy objects using the `Ti.UI.Clipboard.setObject()` method. There are two methods we are utilizing in order to copy data to and from the clipboard, `setText()` and `getText()`, which do exactly the function they both describe. We are setting the text in the clipboard from our first text field using the **Copy** button, and then pasting that same text programmatically into the second text field using the **Paste** button. Using the clipboard has many uses, but the most important one is its ability to let users share data provided by your application with other applications on their device (as seen in the following screenshots). As an example, you may provide a "copy" button for an e-mail address that can then be copied and pasted by the user into their local e-mail client, such as Mobile Mail or Google Gmail.

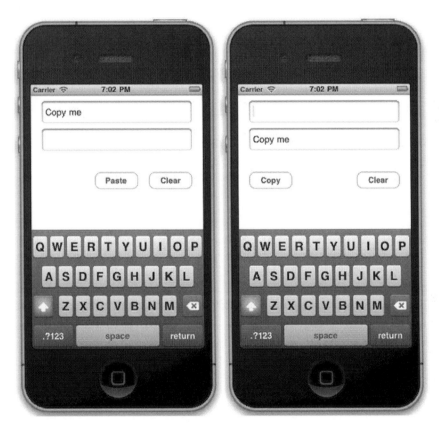

Creating a background service on the iPhone

Apple now supports background services in iOS 4 and above, meaning your apps can now run code in the background much like Android apps are able to. In this recipe we are going to create a background service, which will execute a set piece of code from a separate file called `bg.js`. We will also log each stage of the background service cycle to the console so you can understand each process.

 Complete source code for this recipe can be found in the `/Chapter 8/Recipe 4` folder.

How to do it...

Open your project's `app.js` file in your IDE and enter in the following code (deleting any existing code):

```
//create root window
var win1 = Titanium.UI.createWindow({
  backgroundColor: '#fff',
  title: 'Background Services'
});


function validiOSPlatform() {
  //add iphone checks
  if (Titanium.Platform.osname == 'iphone')
  {
    var version = Titanium.Platform.version.split(".");
    var major = parseInt(version[0],0);

    //can only test this support on ios 4+
    if (major >= 4) {
      return true;
    }
  }

  //either we're not running ios or platform is old
  return false;
}
```

```
if (validiOSPlatform() == true) {
  //register a background service.
  //this JS will run when the app is backgrounded
  var service =
  Ti.App.iOS.registerBackgroundService({url:'bg.js'});

  Ti.API.info("registered background service = " + service);

  //fired when an app is resuming for suspension
  Ti.App.addEventListener('resume',function(e){
    Ti.API.info("App is resuming from the background");
  });

  //fired when an app has resumed
  Ti.App.addEventListener('resumed',function(e){
    Ti.API.info("App has resumed from the background");
  });

  //fired when an app is paused
  Ti.App.addEventListener('pause',function(e){
    Ti.API.info("App was paused from the foreground");
  });
}



//finally, open the window
win1.open();
```

Now create a new file called `bg.js` and save it to your project's `Resources` folder, then type in the following code. This is the code we are going to execute via our background service:

```
Ti.API.info("This line was executed from a background service!");
```

When finished, run your application in the emulator to test it.

How it works...

There are two major steps being undertaken with this recipe. The first is ensuring that the device we're currently running is indeed an iPhone (iOS) device, and second, that it is running the required iOS 4+ operating system. The `validiOSPlatform()` function performs this task and returns a simple Boolean true/false response which indicates whether to proceed with registering our background service or not.

The second part is registering our background service using the file `bg.js` as the code we wish to execute when the application becomes "backgrounded". In this situation, the code in our background service file will fire and log an information message to the console. All of the application pause and resume event listeners are also handled in this example. Therefore, you can run the application in the emulator, open it, exit it, and re-open it again to see each of the event handler fire, and log the matching message to the console.

```
[INFO] One moment, building ...
[INFO] Titanium SDK version: 1.6.3
[INFO] iPhone Device family: iphone
[INFO] iPhone SDK version: 4.3
[INFO] iPhone simulated device: iphone
[INFO] Launching application in Simulator
[INFO] Launched application in Simulator (2.75 seconds)
[INFO] Application started
[INFO] NativeAPIs/1.0 (1.6.3.afce8aa...)
[INFO] registered background service = [object TiAppiOSBackgroundService]
[INFO] App was paused from the foreground
[INFO] This line was executed from a background service!
[INFO] App is resuming from the background
[INFO] App has resumed from the background
```

Displaying local notifications on the iPhone

Another post iOS 4+ feature was the introduction of local notifications which allowed the developer to create basic notification alerts that looked and acted similar to **Push** notifications, but without the hassle of creating all of the certificates and server-side code necessary for Push to work. In this recipe, we are going to extend the previous code that we wrote for our background service, and create a local notification when the app is pushed to the background of the system.

 Complete source code for this recipe can be found in the `/Chapter 8/Recipe 5` folder.

How to do it...

Open your project's `bg.js` file from the previous recipe, and extend it by adding in the following code:

```
var notification = Ti.App.iOS.scheduleLocalNotification({
    alertBody: 'Hey, this is a local notification!',
    alertAction: "Answer it!",
```

```
      userInfo: {"Hello": "world"},
      date: new Date(new Date().getTime())
   });
```

Now in your `app.js` file, create the following event listener and handler. It will execute whenever your **Answer It** confirmation button is pushed during the background process:

```
//listen for a local notification event
Ti.App.iOS.addEventListener('notification', function(e)
   {
      Ti.API.info("Local notification received: "+ JSON.stringify(e));
      alert('Your local notification caused this event to fire!');
   });
```

When you are finished, run your application in the emulator to test it. You should be able to "background", or pause, the application after it starts running (by pressing the "home" button on your iPhone) and receive a local notification. Tapping on **Answer It** will reload your app and cause our "notification' event listener to fire (as seen in the following screenshots)!

How it works...

A local notification consists of a number of parameters, including:

- `alertBody`: The message that appears in your alert dialog
- `alertAction`: The right-hand button that executes your application
- `userInfo`: The data you wish to pass back to your app
- `date`: When to execute the notification

Our example is using the current date and time, meaning the notification will appear momentarily after the application has become "backgrounded". When the notification appears, the user can then either cancel it, or use our custom "action" button to re-launch the app and execute our "notification" event handler.

Displaying Android notifications using intents

Intents are the Android terminology for an operation that is to be performed on the system. Most significantly, it is used for launching activities. The primary parameters of an intent are:

1. The "action": A general action to be performed, such as `ACTION_VIEW`
2. The "data": The data to operate the action on, such as database record or contact person data

In this recipe we are going to use intents in conjunction with Android's Notification Manager in order to create a local notification which will appear in our user's Android notification bar.

 Complete source code for this recipe can be found in the `/Chapter 8/Recipe 6` folder.

How to do it...

You will need the package identifier (in the format of *com.yourcompany.yourapp*—you can find it on the **Edit** tab in Titanium Studio) and the class name of your Android app. You can find the class name by opening the `Build/Android` folder in your project, and then opening the `Android.manifest.xml` file contained within. Under the `application` node you will find a section that looks like the following:

```
<activity
  android:name=".NativeapisActivity"
  android:label="NativeAPIs"
```

```
    android:theme="@style/Theme.Titanium"
    android:configChanges="keyboardHidden|orientation"
>

    ...
```

Your `className` property is a combination of your application identifier and the `android:name` attribute in the previous XML. In our case, this `className` property is `com.boydlee.nativeapis.NativeapisActvitity`.

With these two values written down, open your project's `app.js` file in your IDE and enter in the following code (deleting any existing):

```
//create root window
var win1 = Titanium.UI.createWindow();

if(Titanium.Platform.osname == 'android')
{
  var intent = Titanium.Android.createIntent({
    action: Titanium.Android.ACTION_MAIN,
    className: 'com.boydlee.nativeapis.NativeapisActivity',
    packageName: 'com.boydlee.nativeapis'
  });

  intent.addCategory(Titanium.Android.CATEGORY_LAUNCHER);

  var pending = Titanium.Android.createPendingIntent({
    activity: Titanium.Android.currentActivity,
    intent: intent,
    type:
    Titanium.Android.PENDING_INTENT_FOR_ACTIVITY,
    flags: Titanium.Android.FLAG_ACTIVITY_NEW_TASK
  });

  var notification =
  Titanium.Android.createNotification({
    contentIntent: pending,
    contentTitle: 'New Notification',
    contentText: 'Hey there Titanium Developer!!',
    tickerText: 'You have a new Titanium message...',
    ledARGB: 1,
    number: 1,
    when: new Date().getTime()
  });
```

```
    Ti.Android.NotificationManager.notify(1,
    notification);
}


    //finally, open the window
    win1.open();
```

When finished, run your application in the Android emulator to test it. Once your application has launched you should be able to then exit and pull down the Android notification bar to see the results.

How it works...

In this recipe we are using intents and activities in conjunction with a notification message. The `notification` object itself is relatively simple. It takes in a number of parameters including the title and message of the notification, along with a badge `number` and `when` parameter (the `datetime` that the notification will show, which we have set to the default value 'now'). The `ledARGB` parameter is the color to flash on the device LED, which we have set to the device default.

You'll notice that we also added a category to our intent, using the `addCategory` method, such as `intent.addCategory(Titanium.Android.CATEGORY_LAUNCHER);`. In our example, we used `CATEGORY_LAUNCHER`, which means that our intent should appear in the Launcher as a top-level application.

Coupled with our notification is an object called `pending`. This is our *intent*, and that intent has been written in order to launch an *activity*. In our case, the activity is to launch our application again. You can also add URL properties to intents so that your application can launch specific code on re-entry.

The following screenshot shows an example of our notification message in action:

Storing your Android app on the device's SD card

One of the downsides to Titanium is that, due to its compilation process, applications built on the Titanium platform tend to be rather large in file size in comparison to a native app. Most simple apps in Titanium will range from between 4-5 megabytes in size. This is not really a problem for an iPhone, but unfortunately many Android devices utilize SD card memory and do not have much in the way of local phone storage space.

In this recipe, we will show you how to configure your Android application in order for it to run on the SD card, via Android's **Move to SD card** button in the application settings screen.

 Complete source code for this recipe can be found in the /Chapter 8/Recipe 7 folder.

How to do it...

Open the `tiapp.xml` file under your project's root directory and find the `<android>` node in the XML which will be located near the bottom of the file. Alter the `<android>` node so it looks like the following code:

```
<android xmlns:android="http://schemas.android.com/apk/res/android">
  <tool-api-level>8</tool-api-level>
  <manifest android:installLocation="preferExternal">
    <uses-sdk android:minSdkVersion="7" />
  </manifest>
</android>
```

Now build and run your application on your Android device. Note that this may not work in the emulator.

How it works...

There are a few important parts to understand in relation to this XML configuration. The first is that the `<tool-api-level>` node value is actually referring to the minimum version of the Android tools required. Version 8 is the minimum needed to enable the external storage functionality.

The `<android:installLocation>` attribute refers to the initial storage of the application upon installation. Here we are telling the Android OS that we prefer it to be stored externally to an SD card. However, if one is unavailable, the app will be stored directly to the phone memory. You can also use a value of `internalOnly`, which would disallow the app from being installed on external memory.

Finally, the `<uses-sdk>` node refers to the version of Android required. Version 7 in this case refers to Android 2.1 and up, which is required in order to perform the **Copy To SD-Card** action.

9
Integrating your Apps with External Services

In this chapter, we will cover:

- ▶ Connecting to APIs that use basic authentication
- ▶ Fetching data from the Google Places API
- ▶ Connecting to FourSquare using OAuth
- ▶ Posting a check-in to FourSquare
- ▶ Searching and retrieving data via Yahoo! YQL
- ▶ Integrating push notifications with UrbanAirship.com
- ▶ Testing push notifications using PHP and HTTP POST

Introduction

Many mobile applications are self-contained programs (such as a Calculator app) and have no need to interact with other services or systems. However, will find that as you build more and more, it will start to become necessary to integrate with external vendors and systems in order to keep your users happy. The recent trend towards integrating Facebook "like" buttons and the ability to Tweet from within an app are excellent examples of this.

In this chapter, we are going to be concentrating on talking to a variety of different service providers in a number of common ways, including basic authorization, open authorization, and using a service provider (such as Urban Airship), coupled with some PHP code, to make push notifications work on your iPhone.

Connecting to APIs that use basic authentication

Basic authentication is a method for gaining access to a system by way of Base64 encoding using the username and password credentials before sending them over HTTP. For example, given the username 'Aladdin' and password 'open sesame', the string 'Aladdin:open sesame' is Base64 encoded, resulting in 'QWxhZGRpbjpvcGVuIHNlc2FtZQ=='. This Base64 string is then decoded by the receiving server, resulting in the original username-password string separated by a colon. While this is not the most secure of authentication schemes, it is unreadable to the human eye, and for small APIs or private systems it is very easily implemented. All web browsers from the HTTP/1.1 support basic authentication, so it can be widely implemented across both the Web and mobile devices without being concerned about browser support.

Many external services use basic authentication and session keys in order for you to access and interact with their APIs. In this example, I will show you how to access the Blurtit API using the basic authentication mechanism. The basic principles of this recipe should work for any other standard API that uses basic authentication as well.

Getting ready

Blurtit is a free online question and answer system, much like Yahoo! Answers, or many of the other Q&A style message boards that are on the Web. You will need to set up an account with Blurtit.com and register for their API, which is at `http://api.blurtit.com`. After registering, you will be given a user ID, API key, login name, and password. You'll need these four items in order to connect to the API and retrieve data.

 The complete source code for this recipe can be found in the `/Chapter 9/Recipe 1` folder.

How to do it...

Create a new project in Titanium Studio, and open up the `app.js` file, removing all of the existing code. First, we'll create some variables which will contain your API key, user ID, username, password, and the URL to the API. Make sure you replace the `loginName` and `loginPassword` variable values in the following code with the login information given to you when you signed up for the API in the *Getting ready* section:

```
var win = Titanium.UI.createWindow();

var userid = '123456';
var apikey = 'B_1a0350b39b19a05************';
```

```
var loginName = 'b****@gmail.com';
var loginPasswd = '******';
var apiUrl = 'http://api.blurtit.com/users/signin.json';
```

Now, to do the basic authentication, we need to create a request header. This information gets sent after your **xhr** httpClient object is declared, but before you execute the send method:

```
var xhr = Titanium.Network.createHTTPClient();

xhr.open('POST', apiUrl);
authstr = 'Basic ' + Titanium.Utils.base64encode(userid+':'+apikey);
xhr.setRequestHeader('Authorization', authstr);
```

Next, create your parameter array based on the Blurtit API. In this case, we're passing in our login_name and password variables to perform a signin request. Attach the params array to your xhr.send() method like so:

```
var params = {
    'login_name': loginName,
    'password': loginPasswd
};
xhr.send(params);
```

Finally, in the xhr.onload() method, read in the responseText and assign it to a JSON object. We can then read in the returned data (in this case, a session ID) and we'll assign it to a label for display purposes:

```
//create and add the label to the window
var lblsession = Titanium.UI.createLabel({
  width: 280,
  height: 'auto',
  textAlign: 'center'
});
win.add(lblsession);

//execute our onload function and assign the result to
//our lblsession control
xhr.onload = function() {
    Titanium.API.info(' Text: ' + this.responseText);
    var jsonObject = JSON.parse(this.responseText);
    lblsession.text = "Session ID: \n" +
    jsonObject.user.session_id;
};

//finally open the window
win.open();
```

Now that we have authorized and stored our session variable, we can call the functions available to us on the Blurtit API. The following is a sample which asks the API a simple question and then logs the JSON response to the console:

```
function callAPI(apiFunction, params)
{
    var xhr = Titanium.Network.createHTTPClient();
    Ti.API.info('Session ID = ' + sessionid);

    xhr.onload = function() {
        //this is the response data to our question
        Titanium.API.info(' Text: ' + this.responseText);
        var jsonObject = JSON.parse(this.responseText);
    };

    xhr.open('POST', apiUrl + apiFunction);
    authstr = 'Basic '+
    Titanium.Utils.base64encode(userid+':'+apikey);
    xhr.setRequestHeader('Authorization', authstr);

    xhr.send(params);
}

var params = {
        'session_id': sessionid,
        'query': "Who is Britney Spears?"
};



    //call the api with your session_id and question_id
    callAPI('questions/search.json?query=' +
            txtQuestion.value, params);
```

How it works...

The basic authentication system works on the principle of authenticating and receiving a session token which can then be used in every following API call as a means of indentifying yourself to the server. This session variable is passed in as a parameter for every call to the system you will make. This can be seen in our previous code where we are calling the search questions method (`questions/search.json?query=xxx`).

It should be noted that security is not the purpose of encoding the username and password variables into a Base64 string. Rather, it is done to ensure that possible non-HTTP compatible characters are encoded into values that are HTTP compatible. The basic authentication method is still widely in use on the Internet. However, it is being replaced with OAuth in many cases today. We will look at integrating with OAuth in one of the next recipes of this chapter.

Fetching data from the Google Places API

The Google Places API is a new part of Google Maps and returns information about places (for example, banks, cash machines, services, airports, and more). It marks an attempt by Google to connect users directly to shops or items of interest near their location, and is heavily geared towards mobile usage. In this recipe, we will create a new module which will contain all of the code required to connect to, and return data from, the Google Places API.

Getting ready

You will require an API key from Google in order to perform requests against the Places API. You can obtain a key from Google's developer website here: `https://code.google.com/apis/console`.

Complete source code for this recipe can be found in the `/Chapter 9/Recipe 2` folder.

How to do it...

Create a new project in Titanium Studio, which you can give any name you want. Then, create a new file called `placesapi.js` file, and save it to your project's `Resources` directory. Type the following code into this new JavaScript file:

```
var api = {
    xhr: null
};

var places = (function() {
  //create an object which will be our public API
  //data format must be json or xml
  api.getData = function(lat, lon, radius, types, name, sensor,
success, error) {
    if(api.xhr == null){
```

```
            api.xhr = Titanium.Network.createHTTPClient();
        }

    var url =
    "https://maps.googleapis.com/maps/api/place/search/json?";
    url = url + "location=" + lat + ',' + lon;
    url = url + "&radius=" + radius;
    url = url + "&types=" + types;
    url = url + "&name=" + name;
    url = url + "&sensor=" + sensor;
    url = url + "&key="
    + Titanium.App.Properties.getString("googlePlacesAPIKey");
     Ti.API.info(url);

    api.xhr.open('GET', url);
    api.xhr.setRequestHeader('Content-Type', 'application/json;
charset=utf-8');

     api.xhr.onerror = function(e){
         Ti.API.error("API ERROR " + e.error);
         if (error) {
             error(e);
         }
     };

     api.xhr.onload = function(){
         Ti.API.debug("API response: " + this.responseText);
         if (success) {
             var jsonResponse = JSON.parse(this.responseText);
             success(jsonResponse);
         }
     };

     api.xhr.send();
};

    //data format must be json or xml
    api.getPlaceDetails = function(reference, sensor, success,
                         error) {
        if(api.xhr == null){
            api.xhr = Titanium.Network.createHTTPClient();
        }

    var url =
    "https://maps.googleapis.com/maps/api/place/details/json?";
```

```
url = url + "reference=" + reference;
url = url + "&sensor=" + sensor;
url = url + "&key=" +
Titanium.App.Properties.getString("googlePlacesAPIKey");

//for debugging should you wish to check the URL
//Ti.API.info(url);

  api.xhr.open('GET', url);
  api.xhr.setRequestHeader('Content-Type', 'application/json;
  charset=utf-8');

    api.xhr.onerror = function(e){
        Ti.API.error("API ERROR " + e.error);
        if (error) {
            error(e);
        }
    };

    api.xhr.onload = function(){
        Ti.API.debug("API response: " + this.responseText);
        if (success) {
            var jsonResponse = JSON.parse(this.responseText);
            success(jsonResponse);
        }
    };

    api.xhr.send();
};

//return our public API
return api;

} ());
```

Now open your `app.js` file (or wherever you intend to call the Places module from), removing all of the existing code. Type in the following sample code in order to get data back using our API wrapper. Note that you can return XML data from this API in this example only using JSON, which should really be your de-facto standard for any mobile development. You will also need to replace the XXXXXXXXXXXXXXXXXXXX API key with your own valid API key from Google.

```
//include our placesapi.js module we created earlier
Ti.include('placesapi.js');

//Types array
var types = ['airport', 'atm', 'bank', 'bar', 'parking', 'pet_store',
'pharmacy', 'police', 'post_office', 'shopping_mall'];
```

```
Titanium.App.Properties.setString("googlePlacesAPIKey", "XXXXXXXXXXXXX
XXXXXXXXXXXXXXXXXXXX");

//fetch banks and atm's
//note the types list is a very short sample of all the types of
//places available to you in the Places API
places.getData(-33.8670522, 151.1957362, 500, types[1] + "|" +
types[2], '', 'false',
function(response) {
    //getting an item out of the json response
    Ti.API.info(response.results[1].name);
    Ti.API.info(response.results[1].vicinity);
    Ti.API.info(response.results[1].icon);
    Ti.API.info(response.results[1].types[0]);
},
function(e) {
    Titanium.UI.createAlertDialog({
        title: "API call failed",
        message: e,
        buttonNames: ['OK']
    }).show();
});
```

Run the sample application in the emulator and you should be able to get a JSON formatted list returned, and the first item in that list logged to the console. Try extending this sample to integrate with Google Maps using real-time location data! You can also get more detailed place information by calling the `getPlaceDetails()` method of the API, for example:

```
places.getPlaceDetails(response.results[1].reference, 'false',
function(response){
    //log the json response to the console
    Ti.API.info(response);
},
function(e){
    //something went wrong
    //log any errors etc…
});
```

How it works...

The Places API is probably the simplest kind of service integration available. With it, there is no authentication method except requiring an API key and all of the parameters are passed via the query string using a HTTP GET.

The request header is one important feature of this method. Note that we need to set the content type to `application/json` before performing our `send()` call on the xhr object. Without setting the content type you run the risk of the data being returned to you in HTML or some other format that won't be 100 percent JSON compatible. Therefore, it would probably not load into a JSON object.

When the Places service returns JSON results from a search, it places them within a results array. Even if the service returns no results, it still returns an empty results array. Each element of the response contains a single place result from the area you specified by the latitude and longitude inputs, ordered by prominence. Many things, including the number of check-ins, can affect the prominence of results and therefore its popularity. The Google documentation provides the following information on the data returned for each place result (see `http://code.google.com/apis/maps/documentation/places/`):

- **name** contains the human-readable name for the returned result. For **establishment** results, this is usually the business name.

- **vicinity** contains a feature name of a nearby location. This feature often refers to a street or neighborhood within the given results.

- **types[]** contains an array of feature types describing the given result.

- **geometry** contains geometry information about the result, generally including the **location** (geocode) of the Place and (optionally) the **viewport** identifying its general area of coverage.

- **icon** contains the URL of a recommended icon, which may be displayed to the user when indicating this result.

- **reference** contains a unique token that you can use to retrieve additional information about this place. You can store this token and use it at any time in the future to refresh cached data about this Place, but the same token is not guaranteed to be returned for any given Place across different searches.

- **id** contains a unique stable identifier denoting this place.

There are many other features within the Places API, including the ability to "check-in" to a place and more. Additionally, you should also note that when including this recipe into a live application, part of Google's terms is that you must show the "powered by Google" logo in your application, unless the results you're displaying are already on a Google–branded map.

Connecting to FourSquare using OAuth

Open Authorization (known normally by its shortened name, OAuth) is an open standard developed for authorization, which allows a user to share private data stored on one site or device (e.g. your mobile phone) with another site. Instead of using credentials such as a username and password, OAuth relies on tokens instead. Each token has encoded within in it a series of details for a specific site (e.g. FourSquare or Twitter), using specific resources or permissions (for example, photos or your personal information) for a specific duration of time (for example, two hours).

FourSquare is a popular location-based social networking site specifically made for GPS-enabled mobile devices. It allows you to check-in to various locations, and in doing so, earn points and rewards in the form of "badges". In this recipe, we will use OAuth to connect to FourSquare and retrieve an access token that we can use later on to enable our application to "check-in" to various locations within the FourSquare community.

Getting ready

You will need a Client ID key from FourSquare in order to perform requests against the FourSquare API. You can obtain a key from the developer website for free here: `http://developer.foursquare.com`.

 The complete source code for this recipe can be found in the /Chapter 9/Recipe 3 folder.

How to do it...

Create a new project in Titanium Studio, which you can give any name you want. Then, create a new file called `fsq_module.js` and save it to your projects `Resources` directory. This file will contain all of the needed source code to create a module that we can include anywhere in our Titanium app. Open your new `fsq_module.js` file in your editor and type in the following:

```
var FOURSQModule = {};

(function() {
    FOURSQModule.init = function(clientId, redirectUri) {
        FOURSQModule.clientId = clientId;
        FOURSQModule.redirectUri = redirectUri;
        FOURSQModule.ACCESS_TOKEN = null;
        FOURSQModule.xhr = null;
        FOURSQModule.API_URL = "https://api.foursquare.com/v2/";
    };
```

```
    FOURSQModule.logout = function() {
        showAuthorizeUI(
        String.format('https://foursquare.com/oauth2/
authorize?response_type=token&client_id=%s&redirect_uri=%s',
        FOURSQModule.clientId,
        FOURSQModule.redirectUri)
        );
        return;
    };

    /**
    * displays the familiar web login dialog
    *
    */
    FOURSQModule.login = function(authSuccess_callback) {

        if (authSuccess_callback != undefined) {
            FOURSQModule.success_callback = authSuccess_callback;
        }

        showAuthorizeUI(
        String.format('https://foursquare.com/oauth2/
authenticate?response_type=token&client_id=%s&redirect_uri=%s',
        FOURSQModule.clientId,
        FOURSQModule.redirectUri)
        );
        return;
    };


    FOURSQModule.closeFSQWindow = function() {
        destroyAuthorizeUI();
    };

    /*
    * display the familiar web login dialog
    */
    function showAuthorizeUI(pUrl)
    {
        window = Ti.UI.createWindow({
            modal: true,
            fullscreen: true,
            width: '100%'
        });
        var transform = Ti.UI.create2DMatrix().scale(0);
        view = Ti.UI.createView({
            top: 5,
            width: '100%',
```

```
        height: 450,
        border: 10,
        backgroundColor: 'white',
        borderColor: '#aaa',
        borderRadius: 20,
        borderWidth: 5,
        zIndex: -1,
        transform: transform
    });
    closeLabel = Ti.UI.createLabel({
        textAlign: 'right',
        font: {
            fontWeight: 'bold',
            fontSize: '12pt'
        },
        text: '(X)',
        top: 5,
        right: 12,
        height: 14
    });
    window.open();

    webView = Ti.UI.createWebView({
        top: 25,
        width: '100%',
        url: pUrl,
        autoDetect: [Ti.UI.AUTODETECT_NONE]
    });
    Ti.API.debug('Setting:[' + Ti.UI.AUTODETECT_NONE + ']');
    webView.addEventListener('beforeload',
    function(e) {
        if (e.url.indexOf('http://www.foursquare.com/') != -1) {
            Titanium.API.debug(e);
            authorizeUICallback(e);
            webView.stopLoading = true;
        }
    });
    webView.addEventListener('load', authorizeUICallback);
    view.add(webView);

    closeLabel.addEventListener('click', destroyAuthorizeUI);
    view.add(closeLabel);

    window.add(view);
```

```
        var animation = Ti.UI.createAnimation();
        animation.transform = Ti.UI.create2DMatrix();
        animation.duration = 500;
        view.animate(animation);
    };


    /*
     * unloads the UI used to have the user authorize the application
     */
    function destroyAuthorizeUI()
    {
        Ti.API.debug('destroyAuthorizeUI');
        // if the window doesn't exist, exit
        if (window == null) {
            return;
        }

        // remove the UI
        try
        {
            Ti.API.debug('destroyAuthorizeUI:webView.
removeEventListener');
            webView.removeEventListener('load', authorizeUICallback);
            Ti.API.debug('destroyAuthorizeUI:window.close()');
            window.hide();
        }
        catch(ex)
        {
            Ti.API.debug('Cannot destroy the authorize UI.
Ignoring.');
        }
    };


    /*
     * fires and event when login fails
     */
    function authorizeUICallback(e)
    {
        Ti.API.debug('authorizeUILoaded ' + e.url);
        Titanium.API.debug(e);

        if (e.url.indexOf('#access_token') != -1)
        {
```

```
                        var token = e.url.split("=")[1];
                        FOURSQModule.ACCESS_TOKEN = token;
                        Ti.App.fireEvent('app:4square_token', {
                            data: token
                        });

                        if (FOURSQModule.success_callback != undefined) {
                            FOURSQModule.success_callback({
                                access_token: token,
                            });
                        }

                        destroyAuthorizeUI();

                    } else if ('http://foursquare.com/' == e.url) {
                        Ti.App.fireEvent('app:4square_logout', {});
                        destroyAuthorizeUI();
                    } else if (e.url.indexOf('#error=access_denied') != -1) {
                        Ti.App.fireEvent('app:4square_access_denied', {});
                        destroyAuthorizeUI();
                    }
                };

    })();
```

Now, back in your `app.js` file, type in the following code to include the new FourSquare module and execute the sign-in function:

```
function loginSuccess(e) {
 alert('You have successfully logged into 4SQ!");
};

FOURSQModule.init('yourclientid', 'http://www.yourfoursquareurl.com');
    FOURSQModule.login(loginSuccess, function(e) {
        Titanium.UI.createAlertDialog({
            title: "LOGIN FAILED",
            message: e,
            buttonNames: ['OK']
        }).show();
    });
```

Try running your application in either the Android or iPhone emulator. You should get a login screen appear on startup that looks similar to the one in the following screenshot:

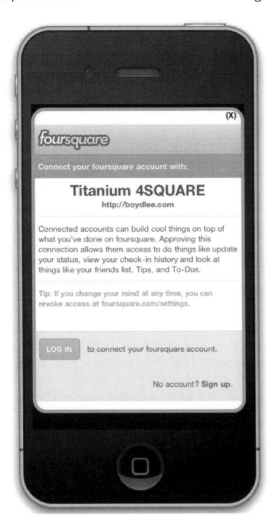

How it works...

The module we have built in this recipe follows a pattern and style that is very similar to others found on the Web, including modules that have been built for Titanium against Facebook, Twitter, and others. It consists of creating a modal view that "pops" up over top of the existing window, and contains a webview to the mobile version of the FourSquare login page. Once the user has logged into the system, we can then grab the access token from the response in the `authorizeCallBack()` method, and save the resulting token to our module's `ACCESS_TOKEN` property.

Posting a check-in to FourSquare

Now that we have created the basic module in order to authenticate against FourSquare, we are going to extend it in order to let the user "check-in" to a particular location. This works by sending details of your current place (for example, a bar, cinema, park, or museum) along with its latitude and longitude values to the FourSquare servers. From there, you can then tell which of your friends are nearby, or alternatively, make your location and activities public for everyone to see.

 Complete source code for this recipe can be found in the /Chapter 9/Recipe 4 folder.

How to do it...

Open your fsq_module.js file and extend the existing module so that it has the extra method as follows:

```
FOURSQModule.callMethod = function(method, GETorPOST, params, success,
error) {
        //get the login information
        try {

            if (FOURSQModule.xhr == null) {
                FOURSQModule.xhr = Titanium.Network.
createHTTPClient();
            }


            FOURSQModule.xhr.open(GETorPOST, FOURSQModule.API_URL +
method + "?oauth_token=" + FOURSQModule.ACCESS_TOKEN);

            FOURSQModule.xhr.onerror = function(e) {
                Ti.API.error("FOURSQModule ERROR " + e.error);
                Ti.API.error("FOURSQModule ERROR " + FOURSQModule.xhr.
location);
                if ( error ) {
                            error(e);
                    }
            };

            FOURSQModule.xhr.onload = function(_xhr) {
                Ti.API.debug("FOURSQModule response: " + FOURSQModule.
xhr.responseText);
                if ( success ) {
```

```
                              success(FOURSQModule.xhr);
                       }
              };

              FOURSQModule.xhr.send(params);
          } catch(err) {
              Titanium.UI.createAlertDialog({
                   title: "Error",
                   message: String(err),
                   buttonNames: ['OK']
              }).show();
          }
     };
```

Now back in your `app.js` file, we are going to extend the "login" call we wrote in the previous recipe to now post a FourSquare check-in after a successful authorization:

```
FOURSQModule.init('yourclientid', 'http://www.yourcallbackurl.com');

FOURSQModule.login(function(e){

       //checkin to a lat/lon location... you can get
       //this from a google map or your GPS co-ordinates
       var params = {
           shout: 'This is my check-in message!',
           broadcast: 'public',
           ll: '33.7,44.2'
       };

       FOURSQModule.callMethod("checkins/add", 'POST', params,
       onSuccess_self, function(e) {
           Titanium.UI.createAlertDialog({
               title: "checkins/add: METHOD FAILED",
               message: e,
               buttonNames: ['OK']
           }).show();
       });

       //now close the foursquare modal window
       FOURSQModule.closeFSQWindow();

   },
   function(event) {
       Titanium.UI.createAlertDialog({
```

```
                    title: "LOGIN FAILED",
                    message: event,
                    buttonNames: ['OK']
            }).show();

        });
```

Now try running your app in the emulator. After logging into the FourSquare system, you should automatically have posted a test check-in titled "This is my check-in message!" and the FourSquare system should send you a successful response message and log it to the console.

How it works...

The `callMethod()` function of our FourSquare module does all of the work here. It is essentially taking in the method name to call, along with whether it is a GET or POST call and the parameters required to make that method work. Our example code is calling the `checkins/add` method, which is a POST, and passing it through the parameters of `shout`, `broadcast`, and `11`. These are our message, privacy setting, and current location respectively. All of the authorization work, including saving our access token, is done via the previous recipe. The following console output shows our response from FourSquare after a successful checkin post:

```
[DEBUG] destroyAuthorizeUI

[DEBUG] destroyAuthorizeUI:webView.removeEventListener

[DEBUG] destroyAuthorizeUI:window.close()

[DEBUG] FOURSQModule response: {"notifications":[{"type":"notification
Tray","item":{"unreadCount":0}},{"type":"message"
,"item":{"message":"OK, got your shout (This is my check-in message!)!
"}}],"response":{"checkin":{"i
d":"4ebf9a5d7ee54e4cd299b72e","createdAt":1321179741,"type":"shout","s
hout":"This is my check-in mes
sage!","timeZone":"Asia/Baghdad","location":{"lat":33.7,"lng":44.2}}}}
```

Searching and retrieving data via Yahoo! YQL

YQL is an SQL-like language that allows you to query, filter, and combine data from multiple sources across both the Yahoo! Network and other open data sources. Normally, developer access to data from multiple resources is disparate and requires calls to multiple APIs from different providers, often with varying feed formats. YQL eliminates this problem by providing a single endpoint to query and shape the data you request. You may remember that we briefly touched on the usage of YQL via standard HTTP Request calls in *Chapter 2*, however, in this chapter, we will be utilizing the built-in Titanium YQL methods.

Titanium has built-in support for YQL, and in this recipe we will create a simple application that searches for stock data on the YQL network, and then displays that data in a simple label.

> Note that when using YQL in an un-authenticated manner (such as we are doing here), there is a usage limit imposed of 100,000 calls per day. For most applications, this is a more than generous limit. However, if you do wish to have it increased, you will need to authenticate your calls via OAuth. You can do this by signing up with Yahoo! and registering your application.

The complete source code for this recipe can be found in the /Chapter 9/Recipe 5 folder.

How to do it...

Create a new project, and then open the app.js file, removing any existing content. Now type in the following code:

```
//
// create base UI tab and root window
//
var win1 = Titanium.UI.createWindow({
    backgroundColor:'#fff'
});

// This is the input textfield for our stock code
var txtStockCode = Titanium.UI.createTextField({
    hintText: 'Stock code, e.g. APPL',
    borderWidth: 0,
    width: 200,
    left: 10,
    height: 30,
    font: {fontSize: 14, fontColor: '#262626'},
    autoCorrect: false,
    autocapitalization: Titanium.UI.TEXT_AUTOCAPITALIZATION_ALL,
    borderStyle: 1,
    top: 5
});

//add the text field to the window
win1.add(txtStockCode);

// Create the search button from our search.png image
var btnSearch = Titanium.UI.createButton({
```

```
        title: 'Search YQL',
        width: 80,
        height: 30,
        right: 10,
        borderRadius: 3,
        top: 5
});

//add the button to the window
win1.add(btnSearch);

//This function is called on search button tap
//it will query YQL for our stock data
function searchYQL() {

  // Do some basic validation to ensure the user
  //has entered a stock code value
  if(txtStockCode.value != '')
  {
    txtStockCode.blur(); //hides the keyboard

    // Create the query string using a combination of
    //YQL syntax and the value of the txtStockCode field
    var query = 'select * from yahoo.finance.quotes where symbol
               = "' + txtStockCode.value + '"';

    // Execute the query and get the results
    Titanium.Yahoo.yql(query, function(e) {
        var data = e.data;
        //Iff ErrorIndicationreturnedforsymbolchangedinvalid
        //is null then we found a valid stock

      if(data.quote.ErrorIndicationreturnedforsymbolchangedinvalid
       == null)
      {
          //show our results in the console
          Ti.API.info(data);

        var lblStockInfo = Titanium.UI.createLabel({
            top: 60,
            left: 20,
            width: 280,
            height: 'auto',
            text: ''
```

```
        });

            //create a label to show some of our info
            lblStockInfo.text = lblStockInfo.text
              + 'Company name: ' + data.quote.Name;
            lblStockInfo.text = lblStockInfo.text +'\nDays Low: '
              + data.quote.DaysLow;
            lblStockInfo.text = lblStockInfo.text +'\nDays High: '
              + data.quote.DaysHigh;
            lblStockInfo.text = lblStockInfo.text +'\nLast Open: '
              + data.quote.Open;
            lblStockInfo.text = lblStockInfo.text +'\nLast Close: '
              + data.quote.PreviousClose;
            lblStockInfo.text = lblStockInfo.text +'\nVolume: '
              + data.quote.Volume;

            win1.add(lblStockInfo);

    }
        else
        {
            //show an alert dialog saying nothing could be found
            alert('No stock information could be found for ' +
txtStockCode.value);
        }
    });

  } //end if
}


// Add the event listener for this button
btnSearch.addEventListener('click', searchYQL);


//open the window
win1.open();
```

You should now be able to run the app in your emulator and search for a stock symbol (such as 'AAPL' for Apple Inc.), and have some of the results listed out to a label on the screen, as seen next:

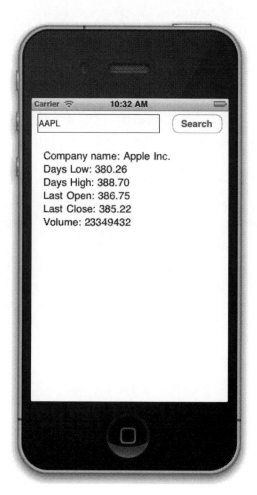

How it works...

What is actually going on here within the searchYQL() function? First, we're doing a very basic validation on the text field to ensure the user has entered in a stock symbol before pressing search. If a stock symbol is found, we use the blur() method of the text field to ensure the keyboard becomes hidden. The meat of the code revolves around creating a Yahoo! YQL query using the correct syntax and providing the text field value as the symbol parameter. This YQL query is simply a string, joined together using the + symbol, much like you would do with any other string manipulation in JavaScript.

We then execute our query using the `Titanium.Yahoo.yql()` method, which returns the results within the 'e' object of the inline response function. We can then manipulate and use this JSON data in any way we wish. In this case, we're assigning a subsection of it to a label on the screen so the user can view the daily opening and closing figures of the stock in question.

Integrating push notifications with UrbanAirship.com

Push notifications is a constantly-open IP connection used to forward notifications from the servers of third party applications to your iOS device. They are used as an alternative to "always running" applications, and allow your device to receive notifications from a specific app even when it is not running. If you have ever received an SMS on your iPhone, then you'll aready know what push notifications looks like. They are essentially a message box that consists of a title, a message, and both a "Close" button and an "Action" button. The "Action" button can be defined by your code, in both appearance and the underlying action and data that you want to be passed to your application when that button is pushed.

Getting ready

You will need to register for an account with Urban Airship at `https://go.urbanairship.com/accounts/register/`. Once you have registered and verified your account via the email link sent to you from Urban Airship, you will need to add a new app to your account at `https://go.urbanairship.com/apps/`. If you haven't already done so, create and download a new Apple Push Certificate from your Apple Developer account. You can do this by creating a new App ID under "Provisioning" in your iOS Developer account, and then in the list of apps find the one you just created, and click on the "configure" link.

A new page should then show up and allow you to select the push notifications option, such as the one in the following screenshot:

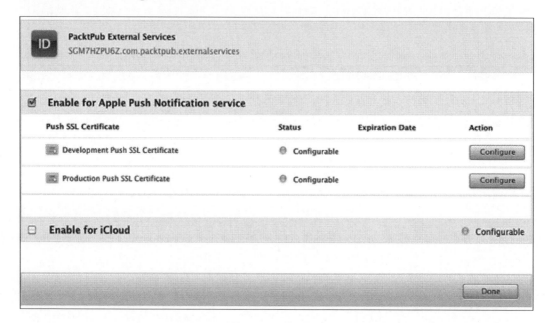

You will need to create an application-specific client SSL certificate, which can be done through keychain. Click on the **Configure** button next to the **Development SSL Certificate** option, and work through the step-by-step wizard. When it is finished, you should be able to download a new Apple Push Notification certificate.

Save this certificate to your computer's hard drive and then double-click the saved file to open it in Keychain Access. In Keychain Access, click on **My Certificates**, and then find the new Apple Push Notification certificate you just created, right-click on it, and select **Export**. You will need to give your new P12 certificate a name. After clicking **Save** you'll also be asked to provide a password, as seen in the following screenshot. This can be anything you like, such as **packt**.

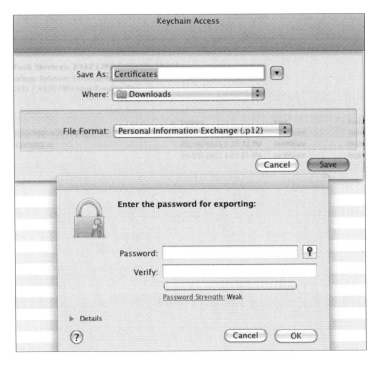

Now go back to the Urban Airship page where you are creating your new application and upload the new P12 certificate, providing the password in the box as requested. Save your application and you are now ready to send push notifications!

 The complete source code for this recipe can be found in the /Chapter 9/Recipe 6 folder.

How to do it...

Create a new development provisioning profile for your application in the provisioning section of the Developer website, and download it to your computer. Next, create a new Titanium project and ensure the app identifier you use matches the identifier you just used to create the provisioning certificate in the Developer Portal. Urban Airship has already created a basic registration sample for you, so we are also going to use that.

Next, open the `app.js` file, removing any existing content. Type in the following code:

```
//create root window
var win = Titanium.UI.createWindow({
    title:'sample',
    backgroundColor:'#fff'
});
```

```
var key = 'your app key';
var secret = 'your app secret';

Titanium.Network.registerForPushNotifications({
    types:[
        Titanium.Network.NOTIFICATION_TYPE_BADGE,
        Titanium.Network.NOTIFICATION_TYPE_ALERT,
        Titanium.Network.NOTIFICATION_TYPE_SOUND
    ],
    success: successCallback,
    error: errorCallback,
    callback: messageCallback
});

function successCallback(e) {
    var request = Titanium.Network.createHTTPClient({
        onload:function(e) {
            if (request.status != 200 && request.status != 201) {
                request.onerror(e);
                return;
            }
        },
        onerror:function(e) {
            alert("Register with Urban Airship Push Service failed.
Error: "
                + e.error);
        }
    });

    // Register device token with UA
    request.open('PUT', 'https://go.urbanairship.com/api/device_
tokens/'
        + e.deviceToken, true);
    request.setRequestHeader('Authorization','Basic '  +
        Titanium.Utils.base64encode(key + ':' + secret));
    request.send();
}

function errorCallback(e) {
    alert("Error during registration: " + e.error);
}

function messageCallback(e) {
    var message;
    if(e['aps'] != undefined) {
        if(e['aps']['alert'] != undefined){
            if(e['aps']['alert']['body'] != undefined){
                message = e['aps']['alert']['body'];
            } else {
```

```
                    message = e['aps']['alert'];
                }
            } else {
                message = 'No Alert content';
            }
        } else {
            message = 'No APS content';
        }
        alert(message);
    }
    //finally, open root window
    win.open();
```

Now, in order to test this code, you must run the application on a device. The emulator simply does not have the push capability and so will not work for this recipe. Go to the **Run on Device** tab in Titanium Studio and provide the screen with the debug provision profile you created in the first steps of this recipe. Next, click on the **Install Now** button to compile and push the application package to your device using iTunes.

Once your application has launched on the device and it is running, go to your web browser and, in your Urban Airship's app page, click on **Push** and then **Device Tokens**. Your new token should be listed on this page. If it is not, double check all of your steps again and ensure you are using the correct mobile provisioning profiles to build your app. You can now click on **Send Broadcast** in order to send a sample push notification to your device directly from the Urban Airship website. Try this now, and you should receive a message on your iPhone that looks very similar to the one shown in the following screenshots:

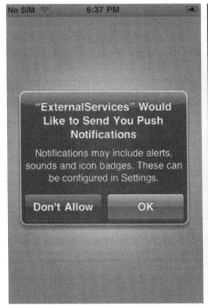 

How it works...

There are a number of key factors in ensuring you are successful in getting Push Notifications to work with your Titanium application. Keep these points in mind:

- ▶ Remember that each application you create needs its own Push Certificate, you cannot use wildcard certificates when integrating Push.

- ▶ Always create the Push Certificate under your Application settings in the developer console first, and then create your provisioning profiles. Doing it the other way around will mean your profile will be invalid and your app will not accept any push notification requests.

- ▶ Push notifications can only be tested on actual iPhone or iPod Touch devices, they will not work under the emulator.

- ▶ The `Titanium.Network.registerForPushNotifications` method requires the types of notifications you wish to use as the first parameter. If you do not request a specific permission from the user upfront, you may not be able to send them that kind of notification in the future. Furthermore, users must always agree to allow you to send push notifications to their device. You will not be able to do so if they do not allow the process to occur.

- ▶ You need to create separate profiles and certificates for push notifications in both the Apple iOS Developer console and Urban Airship. You cannot use a development profile in production and vice versa.

Testing push notifications using PHP and HTTP POST

In order for our server application to programmatically push notifications to a user or group of users, we will need to create a script that can push the notifications to the Urban Airship servers. This can be done in a variety of methods (via desktop app, .NET application, web application and so on), but for the purposes of this recipe we will use PHP, which is simple, fast, and freely available.

 The complete source code for this recipe can be found in the `/Chapter 9/Recipe 7` folder.

How to do it...

First, we need to create the PHP script which will communicate with the Urban Airship servers to send a push notification. Create the following PHP script, save it as `airship.php`, and upload it to a server capable of running PHP and with CURL installed. There are plenty of free PHP/Apache hosting accounts available online if you don't already have one capable of doing this.

The following sample is taken from the Urban Airship website:

```php
<?php
define('APPKEY','xxxx');
define('PUSHSECRET', 'xxx'); // Master Secret
define('PUSHURL',
'https://go.urbanairship.com/api/push/broadcast/');

$contents = array();
$contents['badge'] = "+1";
$contents['alert'] = "Hello there Titanium Developer!";
$push = array("aps" => $contents);

$json = json_encode($push);

$session = curl_init(PUSHURL);
curl_setopt($session, CURLOPT_USERPWD, APPKEY . ':' . PUSHSECRET);
curl_setopt($session, CURLOPT_POST, True);
curl_setopt($session, CURLOPT_POSTFIELDS, $json);
curl_setopt($session, CURLOPT_HEADER, False);
curl_setopt($session, CURLOPT_RETURNTRANSFER, True);
curl_setopt($session, CURLOPT_HTTPHEADER, array('Content-
Type:application/json'));
$content = curl_exec($session);
echo $content; // just for testing what was sent

// Check if any error occured
$response = curl_getinfo($session);
if($response['http_code'] != 200) {
    echo "Got negative response from server, http code: ".
    $response['http_code'] . "\n";
} else {

    echo "Wow, it worked!\n";
}

curl_close($session);
?>
```

All that is left to do now is run the PHP script in a browser, and when you do, you should see a success message echoed out to the browser page, and you should also be able to see a new push notification delivered to your device that was set up in the previous recipe, as seen in the following screenshot:.

How it works...

The PHP script in this recipe is doing much the same job as the actual Urban Airship website does when you can perform tests via their console. Here, we are using PHP to build a CURL request in JSON and post it to the Urban Airship server. That request is in turn received and then pushed out to your device or devices as a Push Notification by the Urban Airship system.

In a production environment, you would want to extend your PHP script to either receive the badge and message variables as POST variables, or perhaps hook up the script directly to a database with whatever business logic your app requires. You should also note that Urban Airship provides samples for languages other than PHP. So if your system is built in .NET or another platform, the same principles of sending out broadcasts still apply.

10
Extending your Apps With Custom Modules

In this chapter, we will cover:

- ▶ Integrating an existing module—the PayPal Mobile Payment Library
- ▶ Preparing your iOS module development environment
- ▶ Developing a new iPhone module using XCode
- ▶ Creating a public API method
- ▶ Packaging and testing your module using the test harness
- ▶ Packaging your module for distribution and sale

Introduction

While Titanium allows you to create apps that are almost cross-platform, it is inevitable that some devices will inherently have operating system and hardware differences that are specific to them (particularly between Android and iOS). For example, anyone who has used both Android and iPhone devices would immediately recognize the very different way the notification systems are set up. However, there are other platform-specific limitations that are very specific to the Titanium API.

In this chapter, we will be discussing both building and integrating modules into your Titanium applications, using the iOS platform as an example. The methods of developing Android modules using Java are very similar, however, for our purposes, we will just be concentrating on developing modules for iOS using Objective-C and XCode.

Integrating an existing module—the PayPal Mobile Payment Library

There are already a number of modules written for the Titanium platform, both by Appcelerator themselves and by the community at large. There is even a brand new Open Mobile Marketplace where you can buy (and sell) modules to extend the platform to even newer and greater heights!

Getting ready

You will first need to sign up for the Titanium + Commerce program before you can download and use the PayPal Mobile Payment Library. You can do this for free at `http://www.appcelerator.com/products/titaniumcommerce/`. Once you have filled in the required form, simply download the ZIP file titled Titanium+Commerce MPL for Paypal Module for iOS to your computer's hard drive.

You must also register your application with PayPal, and on doing so you will be provided with an Application ID that you must reference inside your Titanium project. You can register for an Application ID from `http://www.paypal.com`. Note that the registration of an Application ID also requires you to be a PayPal member, so you may be required to sign up first if you have not already done so in the past.

> The complete source code for this recipe can be found in the `/Chapter 10/Recipe 1` folder.

How to do it...

First, you'll need to copy the Paypal module files to the `modules` folder under your Titanium installation. On OSX, this is normally located at `/Library/Application Support/Titanium/modules`. There should already be a subfolder under modules called "iphone". If there is not, create one now, then unzip the module file so that you end up with a `ti.paypal` folder, located at `/Library/Application Support/Titanium/modules/iphone/ti.paypal`. Take a quick look inside that folder. You should immediately notice that the first subfolder underneath it is named "1.0" or possibly "1.2". This is the version number of the module you just installed. Pay careful attention to note it down as this will be important later on.

Once that is completed, the `tiapp.xml` file for your project needs to be edited so that the modules section includes our `ti.paypal` module. This reference tells the Titanium Studio compiler to add in the module when your project is built. Extend the `tiapp.xml` file by adding the following lines underneath the "guid" element. Make sure the module version number matches the version number of the `ti.paypal` library you just installed.

```
<modules>
    <module version="1.0">ti.paypal</module>
</modules>
```

Now back in your `app.js` file, we need to include the module reference at the top of the JavaScript like so:

```
Ti.Paypal = require('ti.paypal');
```

We can now use this new variable object to create a PayPal payment button object and add it to our window. The PayPal library also includes a number of event listeners to handle payment success, error, and cancellation events. Here is a sample of how you could use the PayPal library to take a payment donation for the American Red Cross, taken from the Appcelerator KitchenSink sample:

```
var ppButton = Ti.Paypal.createPaypalButton({
    width: 294,
    height: 50,
    bottom: 50,
     appId: "YOUR_PAYPAL_APP_ID",
     buttonStyle: Ti.Paypal.BUTTON_294x43,
     paypalEnvironment: Ti.Paypal.PAYPAL_ENV_SANDBOX,
     feePaidByReceiver: false,
     transactionType: Ti.Paypal.PAYMENT_TYPE_DONATION,
     enableShipping: false,
     payment: {
         amount: win.data.amt,
         tax: 0.00,
         shipping: 0.00,
         currency: "USD",
         recipient: "osama@x.com",
         itemDescription: "Donation",
         merchantName: "American Red Cross"
     }
});

ppButton.addEventListener("paymentCanceled", function(e){
    Ti.API.info("Payment Canceled");
});

ppButton.addEventListener("paymentSuccess", function(e){
    Ti.API.info("Success");
    win.fireEvent("completeEvent", {data: win.data, transid:
e.transactionID});
});

ppButton.addEventListener("paymentError", function(e){
    Ti.API.info("Payment Error");

});
```

If you have installed the module correctly and updated your `tiapp.xml` file correctly, you should see a message saying "Detected third-party module: [Module Name]/[Module Version]". In our case, this will say that it has detected the `ti.paypal` module.

The following is an example of the Red Cross app running and using the PayPal module for Titanium. This sample code is available as part of this recipe.

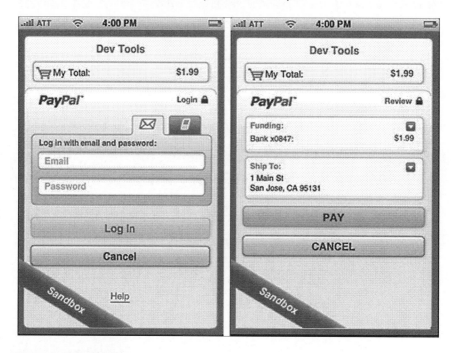

How it works...

Once your module has been copied to the modules directory and referenced in the `tiapp.xml`, you can use it just like any other piece of native Titanium JavaScript. All of the modules public methods and properties have been made available to you by the module's developer.

More specifically to our PayPal module, once the buyer clicks on the "Paypal" purchase button in your app, the Payment checkout process is shown. Whenever an important event occurs (for example, payment success), these events are thrown and caught by Titanium using the event handlers below. Your application needs to incorporate these three handlers:

```
ppButton.addEventListener("paymentCanceled", function(e){
   Titanium.API.info("Payment Canceled");
});

ppButton.addEventListener("paymentSuccess", function(e){
   Titanium.API.info("Payment Success.   TransactionID: " +
```

```
      e.transactionID);
   });

   ppButton.addEventListener("paymentError", function(e){
      Titanium.API.info("Payment Error");
      Titanium.API.info("errorCode: " + e.errorCode);
      Titanium.API.info("errorMessage: " + e.errorMessage);
   });
```

When a payment has been successfully transmitted, a transaction ID will be returned to your "paymentSuccess" event listener. It should be noted that in this example we are using the Paypal Sandbox (Testing) environment, and for a live app you would need to change the `paypalEnvironment` variable to `Ti.PayPal.PAYPAL_ENV_LIVE`. In the sandbox environment, no actual money is transferred.

There's more...

Try experimenting with the different properties made available to you in the PayPal module. Here's a list of the most useful properties and their constant values:

`buttonStyle`	Size and appearance of the PayPal button, the available values are:
	Titanium.Paypal.BUTTON_68x24
	Titanium.Paypal.BUTTON_118x24
	Titanium.Paypal.BUTTON_152x33
	Titanium.Paypal.BUTTON_194x37
	Titanium.Paypal.BUTTON_278x43
	Titanium.Paypal.BUTTON_294x43
`paypalEnvironment`	Available values are:
	Titanium.Paypal.PAYPAL_ENV_LIVE
	Titanium.Paypal.PAYPAL_ENV_SANDBOX
	Titanium.Paypal.PAYPAL_ENV_NONE
`feePaidByReceiver`	This will only be applied when the transaction type is Personal.
	Available values are:
	true
	false

transactionType	The type of payment being made (what the payment is for).
	Available values are:
	Titanium.Paypal.PAYMENT_TYPE_HARD_GOODS
	Titanium.Paypal.PAYMENT_TYPE_DONATION
	Titanium.Paypal.PAYMENT_TYPE_PERSONAL
	Titanium.Paypal.PAYMENT_TYPE_SERVICE
enableShipping	Whether or not to select/send shipping information.
	Available values are:
	true
	false

Preparing your iOS module development environment

Before you can start to develop your own custom iOS modules, you will first need to set up your environment correctly. This involves setting up an alias to the `titanium.py` script in your Titanium SDK path.

Getting ready

The following instructions are for Mac OSX only. It is possible to develop Android modules on Linux and Windows, as well as OSX. However, for this recipe, we will be concentrating on iOS module development, which requires an Apple Mac, running OSX 10.5, or above.

How to do it...

1. Open the **Terminal** application, which you will find under **Applications | Utilities | Terminal**.

2. Type in `cd $HOME` and press *Enter*.

3. Type in `vi .bash_profile` and press *Enter*. If you have not created a `bash_profile` before, then you will be creating a new file now, otherwise it will load your existing `bash_profile` script.

4. Add the following line to your script: `"alias titanium='/Library/Application\ Support/Titanium/mobilesdk/osx/1.7.2/titanium.py'"`—where `1.7.2` is the latest version of the Titanium SDK you currently have installed. Pay careful attention and ensure your Titanium SDK path is correct and the path location is surrounded by single quotation characters.

5. Save the file by pressing the *Esc* key, and then type "`:wq`". This will save your file and then exit the editor.

6. Back in Terminal, type "`source ~/.bash_profile`" and press *Enter*.

7. Now type in "`titanium`" and press *Enter*. If you have set up the script correctly, you will see an output from Appcelerator in your Terminal window like the one seen in the following screenshot.

8. Leave the Terminal window open since it will be required in the next recipes:

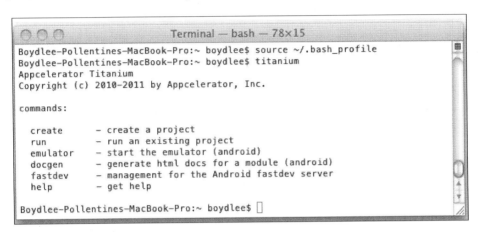

To test that your environment is now set up correctly, type the following into the Terminal window:

```
titanium create --platform=iphone --type=module --dir=~/tmp
--name=test --id=com.packtpub.testmodule
```

If everything has worked, you will see the following output in the Terminal window. You can verify the files this script created by navigating to the `/tmp/test` directory under finder (note that the `tmp` directory will be under your user accounts `Home` folder).

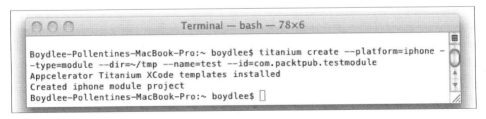

How it works...

Essentially, all we are doing here is setting a way to execute Titanium scripts from the console using an alias. This means we can use simple commands such as "titanium create" instead of attempting to do the same thing manually by executing long-winded commands in the Terminal.

Developing a new iPhone module using XCode

Developing our own custom modules for Titanium allows us to leverage native code and make Titanium do things that it otherwise couldn't, or at least doesn't currently do. For this recipe, we are going to develop a small module that uses Bit.ly to shorten a long URL. You can use this module in any of your iOS apps whenever you need to create a short URL (such as when posting a link to Twitter!).

Getting ready

You will first need to have set up your Mac using the steps described in the previous recipe. Make sure you follow the steps and that your system is set up correctly, as this recipe relies heavily on those scripts working. You will also need some working knowledge of Objective-C for this recipe. This book doesn't try to teach Objective-C in any way as, there are plenty of weighty tomes for that already. However, you should, be able to follow along with the code in this recipe to get our sample module working.

How to do it...

To begin, let's create the basic module using the same script we used in the previous recipe. In the Terminal window, type the following (substituting the /Projects directory for whichever directory you wish to create your module in):

```
titanium create --platform=iphone --type=module --dir=~/Projects
--name=BitlyModule --id=com.packtpub.BitlyModule
```

Now open the /Projects/BitlyModule directory in Finder, and what you will see is a list of mostly standard looking XCode project files. Double click the BitlyModule.xcodeproj file to open it up in XCode for editing.

How it works...

The following information comes straight from the Appcelerator guide (available at `http://wiki.appcelerator.org/display/guides/Module+Developer+Guide+for+iOS`) and is a good introduction to understanding the architecture of a Titanium module.

The Module architecture contains the following key interface components:

1. **Proxy**: A base class that represents the native binding between your JavaScript code and native code.
2. **ViewProxy**: A specialized Proxy that knows how to render Views.
3. **View**: The visual representation of a UI component that Titanium can render.
4. **Module**: A special type of Proxy that describes a specific API set, or namespace.

When building a Module, you can only have one Module class but you can have zero or more Proxies, Views, and `ViewProxies`.

For each `View`, you will need a `ViewProxy`. The `ViewProxy` represents the model data (which is kept inside the proxy itself in case the View needs to be released) and is responsible for exposing the APIs and events that the View supports.

You create a Proxy when you want to return non-visual data between JavaScript and native. The Proxy knows how to handle any method and property dispatching and event firing.

Creating a public API method

The sample module code that Titanium creates as part of its module create process already provides us with a sample of a public method. We are going to create our own though which accepts a single string input value (the "long" URL) and then processes the short URL via the `Bit.ly` API before returning it to our Titanium app.

Getting ready

Before you can use the module, you'll need to sign up for a Bitly API Key, which you can do for free at: `https://bitly.com/a/sign_up?rd=/a/your_api_key`.

Additionally, we're going to need the open source SBJSON framework for Objective-C, which is capable of natively reading and writing JSON formatted data streams. You can download the SBJSON framework from `https://github.com/stig/json-framework/`.

 The complete source code for this recipe can be found in the `/Chapter 10/Recipe 4` folder.

How to do it...

First, unzip the SBJSON framework, and drag all of the files from the `Classes` folder in Finder to the `Classes` folder in your module's XCode project.

Open up `ComPacktpubBitlyModuleModule.h` and ensure it looks like the following (ignoring the header comments at the top of the file):

```
#import "TiModule.h"
#import <Foundation/Foundation.h>

@interface ComPacktpubBitlyModuleModule : TiModule
{
}


@end
```

Now open the `ComPacktpubBitlyModuleModule.m` file and ensure it looks like the following source code (ignoring the header comments at the top of the file). Remember to replace the `login` and `key` values in the `QueryString` section of the URL with those you were assigned by the `Bit.ly` API:

```
#import "ComPacktpubBitlyModuleModule.h"
#import "TiBase.h"
#import "TiHost.h"
#import "TiUtils.h"
#import "SBJson.h"
#import "SBJsonParser.h"

@implementation ComPacktpubBitlyModuleModule

#pragma mark Internal

// this is generated for your module, please do not change it
- (id)moduleGUID
{
    return @"a33e440e-ef62-4ec7-89cd-8939d264e46e";
}

// this is generated for your module, please do not change it
- (NSString*)moduleId
{
    return @"com.packtpub.BitlyModule";
}

#pragma mark Lifecycle

- (void)startup
{
```

```objc
    // this method is called when the module is first loaded
    // you *must* call the superclass
    [super startup];

    NSLog(@"[INFO] %@ loaded",self);
}

-(void)shutdown:(id)sender
{
    // this method is called when the module is being unloaded
    // typically this is during shutdown. make sure you don't
       do too
    // much processing here or the app will be quit forceably

    // you *must* call the superclass
    [super shutdown:sender];
}

#pragma mark Cleanup

-(void)dealloc
{
    // release any resources that have been retained by the module
    [super dealloc];
}

#pragma mark Internal Memory Management

-(void)didReceiveMemoryWarning:(NSNotification*)notification
{
    // optionally release any resources that can be dynamically
    // reloaded once memory is available - such as caches
    [super didReceiveMemoryWarning:notification];
}

#pragma mark Listener Notifications

-(void)_listenerAdded:(NSString *)type count:(int)count
{
    if (count == 1 && [type isEqualToString:@"my_event"])
    {
    // the first (of potentially many) listener is being added
    // for event named 'my_event'
    }
}

-(void)_listenerRemoved:(NSString *)type count:(int)count
{
    if (count == 0 && [type isEqualToString:@"my_event"])
    {
```

```objc
        // the last listener called for event named 'my_event' has
        // been removed, we can optionally clean up any resources
        // since no body is listening at this point for that event
    }
}

#pragma Public APIs

-(id)example:(id)args
{
    // example method
    return @"hello world";
}

///creates the short url from bitly
- (id)getShortUrl:(id)value
{
    NSString *baseURLString = @"http://api.bit.ly/shorten?version=2.0
.1&longUrl=";
    NSString *longUrl = [TiUtils stringValue:value];

    longUrl = [longUrl stringByReplacingOccurrencesOfString:@"("
              withString:@""];
    longUrl = [longUrl stringByReplacingOccurrencesOfString:@")"
              withString:@""];
    longUrl = [longUrl stringByReplacingOccurrencesOfString:@"\""
               withString:@""];
    longUrl = [longUrl
              stringByTrimmingCharactersInSet:[NSCharacterSet
              whitespaceAndNewlineCharacterSet]];
              baseURLString = [baseURLString
              stringByAppendingString:longUrl];

    baseURLString = [baseURLString
    stringByAppendingString:
    @"&login=REPLACE_YOUR_LOGIN&apiKey=REPLACE_YOUR_KEY"];
    NSURL* baseURL = [[NSURL alloc]
        initWithString:baseURLString];

    NSMutableURLRequest *req = [[NSMutableURLRequest alloc]
        initWithURL:baseURL];

    NSHTTPURLResponse* urlResponse = nil;
    NSError *error = [[[NSError alloc] init] autorelease];

    NSData *data = [NSURLConnection sendSynchronousRequest:req
        returningResponse:&urlResponse error:&error];

    if ([urlResponse statusCode] >= 200 && [urlResponse
        statusCode] < 300)
    {
```

```
NSLog(@"Got a response from bit.ly");
  SBJsonParser* jsonParser = [SBJsonParser new];
  NSString* jsonString = [[NSString alloc]
    initWithData:data encoding:NSUTF8StringEncoding];

NSDictionary* dict = (NSDictionary*)[jsonParser
      objectWithString:jsonString];

[jsonString release];
[jsonParser release];

NSString *statusCode = [dict
      objectForKey:@"statusCode"];

if([statusCode isEqualToString:@"OK"])
{
        // retrieve shortURL from results
        NSLog([dict description]);
        NSString *shortURL = [[[dict
            objectForKey:@"results"]
            objectForKey:longUrl]
            objectForKey:@"shortUrl"];
        return shortURL;
}
else
{

    return @"Unable to shorten this URL,
            please check its format.";
}
}

return baseURLString;
}


@end
```

How it works...

The main function here is the one we created, called `getShortUrl`. All other methods and properties for the module have been auto-generated for us by the Titanium module creation scripts. This method, in short, executes a request against the `Bit.ly` API using our key and username, and when a response is received, it is parsed using the SBJSON parser. The resulting `shortURL` variable (of type `NSString`) is then pulled out of the shortURL element of the JSON result, and returned back to Titanium.

What we want to concentrate on here is the integration of the Titanium public method, and how the "value" argument is translated. Here we're using the (id) declaration, which allows us to easily typecast the incoming value to a parameter type that Objective-C understands. In this case, we are typecasting the "value" parameter to a type of `NSString`, as we know the incoming parameter is going to be a string value in the format of a web address. This conversion process is thanks to **TiUtils**, which we've imported at the top of our file using the `#import "TiUtils.h"` command.

Some of the most common conversion examples are:

```
CGFloat f = [TiUtils floatValue:arg];

NSInteger f = [TiUtils intValue:arg];

NSString *value = [TiUtils stringValue:arg];

NSString *value = [TiUtils stringValue:@"key" properties:dict
def:@"default"];

TiColor *bgcolor = [TiUtils colorValue:arg];
```

We are also returning a string value which is either an error message (if the `Bit.Ly` conversion process failed) or, hopefully, the new short URL that `Bit.Ly` has kindly provided us. As we are returning a string, we don't need to perform a conversion before returning the parameter.

The following types can be returned without the need for typecasting:

- `NSString`
- `NSDictionary`
- `NSArray`
- `NSNumber`
- `NSDate`
- `NSNull`

Packaging and testing your module using the test harness

Now it's time to build, package, and test our new module! Before you go ahead with this recipe, make sure you've built the XCode project and it has been successful. If not, you will need to fix any errors before continuing.

 The complete source code for this recipe can be found in the `/Chapter 10/Recipe 5` folder.

How to do it...

Open up the `app.js` example file for our module, you'll find it within the `example` directory of your module project. Replace the existing sample contents with the following source code:

```
// This is a test harness for your module
// You should do something interesting in this harness
// to test out the module and to provide instructions
// to users on how to use it by example.

//  write your module tests here
var bitlymodule = require('com.packtpub.BitlyModule');
Ti.API.info("module is => " + bitlymodule);

// open a single window
var window = Ti.UI.createWindow({
   backgroundColor:'white'
});

var txtLongUrl = Ti.UI.createTextField({
 top: 10,
 left: 10,
 width: 300,
 height: 30,
 borderStyle: 1,
 hintText: 'Enter your long url...'
});
window.add(txtLongUrl);

var btnShorten = Ti.UI.createButton({
 title: 'Shorten it with Bit.ly!',
 width: 200,
 right: 10,
 height: 30,
 top: 50
});
btnShorten.addEventListener('click', function(e){
 var result = bitlymodule.getShortUrl(txtLongUrl.value);
 txtShortUrl.value = result;
});
window.add(btnShorten);

var txtShortUrl = Ti.UI.createTextField({
 top: 100,
 left: 10,
 width: 300,
```

```
    height: 30,
    borderStyle: 1,
    hintText: 'Your short url appears here...'
});
window.add(txtShortUrl);


window.open();
```

Now, back in the Terminal, change directory so that you are in your `BitLyModule` directory (assuming you still have the Terminal window open from a previous recipe, you should already be there).

Type `./build.py` into the Terminal, and press *Enter* to execute the command. When it completes, type `titanium run` and press *Enter*. If all has gone well, you should see the iPhone simulator launch after 20 or 30 seconds, with our example Titanium application visible, which consists of two `TextFields` and the `BitLy` conversion button. Type a long URL into the first `TextField` and press **Shorten it with Bit.ly!** as seen in the following screenshot:

How it works...

Let's concentrate on the Titanium code used to build and launch our module via the example project. As you can see, one of the very first lines in our sample JavaScript is the following:

```
var bitlymodule = require('com.packtpub.BitlyModule');
```

This code instantiates our module, and defines it as a new variable called `bitlymodule`. We can then use our module just like any other regular Titanium control, by calling our own custom method, and returning the result before displaying it in the `shortURL` text field:

```
var result = bitlymodule.getShortUrl(txtLongUrl.value);

txtShortUrl.value = result;
```

Packaging your module for distribution and sale

Titanium modules are created in a way that allows for easy distribution and re-use, both in your own apps or the Titanium+Plus Marketplace. In this recipe, we will go through the steps required to package your module and then distribute it to the marketplace.

 The complete source code for this chapter can be found in the `/Chapter 10` folder, along with the compiled version of the `Bit.Ly` module.

How to do it...

The first requirement is to edit the manifest file that is automatically generated when you created your module. Below is an example taken from our `BitlyModule`:

```
version: 0.1
description: My module
author: Your Name
license: Specify your license
copyright: Copyright (c) 2011 by Your Company

# these should not be edited
name: bitlymodule
moduleid: com.packtpub.BitlyModule
guid: a33e440e-ef62-4ec7-89cd-8939d264e46e
platform: iphone
minsdk: 1.7.2
```

Anything below the `# these should not be edited` line should be left alone, but go ahead and replace all of the other key/value pairs with your own name, description, license, version, and copyright text. Once you have completed editing the manifest file, rebuild your module using by typing `./build.py` into the Terminal, and press *Enter* to execute the command.

Your module is now ready for use in your own projects or for manual distribution. Simply copy the contents of the ZIP file to your copied into the `/Library/Application/ Support/ Titanium` directory for it to be installed. You will of course still need to include your module using the `require` method call in your `app.js` file, and you'll need to reference it in your `tiapp.xml` file as you did in the first recipe of this chapter for the mobile PayPal library.

You can distribute your module to the Open Mobile Marketplace using the same ZIP file package that was created in the build process. However, there are several prerequisites you'll need to fulfill before you can distribute:

1. You must have a valid Titanium developer account.
2. You must have fully completed filling our your manifest values.
3. You must have a valid license text in the LICENSE file in your project.
4. You must have a valid documentation file in the `index.md` file in your documentation directory of your project.
5. You must specify some additional metadata upon upload such as the price (which can be free).
6. If you are charging for your module, you must establish a payment setup with Appcelerator so that you can be paid.
7. You must accept the Titanium+Plus Marketplace terms of service agreement.

Once you have uploaded your module and completed the necessary submission steps, your module will be made available to the marketplace directory. Note that the first time you submit a module Appcelerator will review your module for the basic requirements above.

How it works...

The new Appcelerator marketplace makes it easy for developers to build, sell, and distribute their own custom Titanium modules, for both iOS and Android. All you need to do is set up a profile for your product and provide your PayPal account details in order to be paid for each sale you make.

Developers make 70 percent of all products they sell through the Open Mobile Marketplace, and there are a number of tools available to keep track of your customers, invoices, and feedback. You can sign up today at `https://marketplace.appcelerator.com/cms/landing`.

11

Platform Differences, Device Information, and Quirks

In this chapter, we will cover:

- ▶ Gathering information about your device
- ▶ Obtaining the device's screen dimensions
- ▶ Understanding device orientation modes
- ▶ Coding around differences between the iOS and Android APIs
- ▶ Ensuring your device can make phone calls

Introduction

In this chapter, we are going to go through a number of platform differences between iOS and Android, as well as show you how to code around these differences. We'll also highlight how to gather information about the device your application is running on, including its screen dimensions and capabilities, such as the ability to make a phone call.

 The complete source code for this entire chapter can be found in the /Chapter 11/PlatformDiffs folder.

Gathering information about your device

The majority of information about the current device is available through the `Titanium.Platform` namespace. It is here that we can determine a host of device-specific data, including the battery level, device OS and version, current device language, the screen resolution, and more. Knowing this information is important, as it will give you a series of clues as to what is happening on the physical device. One example is that you may wish to back up a user's application data if the battery dips below a certain percentage, in case the device was to shut down and data was lost. More commonly, you will use device properties such as `Titanium.Platform.osname` to determine what operating system your app is currently running under, such as iPhone, iPad, or Android.

Getting ready

To prepare for this recipe, open up Titanium Studio and log in if you have not already done so. If you need to register a new account, you can do so for free directly from within the application. Once you are logged in, click on **New Project**, and the details window for creating a new project will appear. Enter in **PlatformDiffs** as the name of the app, and fill in the rest of the details with your own information. Open the `app.js` file and remove everything apart from the instantiation of the root window and the `win1` object's open method, so that it looks like the following:

```
//
// create root window
//
var win1 = Titanium.UI.createWindow({
    title:'Tab 1',
    backgroundColor:'#fff'
});

//open root window
win1.open();
```

 The complete source code for this recipe can be found in the `/Chapter 11/Recipe 1` folder.

How to do it...

Now, back in the `app.js` file, we are going to simply create a number of labels and request the values for each from the properties available to us in the `Titanium.Platform` namespace. These values will then be displayed as text on-screen:

```
var labelOS = Titanium.UI.createLabel({
    width:  'auto',
    height: 30,
    top: 0,
    left: 10,
    font: {fontSize: 14, fontFamily: 'Helvetica'},
    color: '#000',
    text: 'OS Details: ' + Titanium.Platform.osname + ' (version ' +
Titanium.Platform.version + ')'
});

var labelBattery = Titanium.UI.createLabel({
    width:  'auto',
    height: 30,
    top: 40,
    left: 10,
    font: {fontSize: 14, fontFamily: 'Helvetica'},
    color: '#000',
    text: 'Battery level: ' + Titanium.Platform.batteryLevel
});

var labelMemory = Titanium.UI.createLabel({
    width:  'auto',
    height: 30,
    top: 80,
    left: 10,
    font: {fontSize: 14, fontFamily: 'Helvetica'},
    color: '#000',
    text: 'Available memory: ' + Titanium.Platform.availableMemory +
'MB'
});

var labelArchitecture = Titanium.UI.createLabel({
    width:  'auto',
    height: 30,
    top: 120,
    left: 10,
    font: {fontSize: 14, fontFamily: 'Helvetica'},
    color: '#000',
    text: 'Architecture: ' + Titanium.Platform.architecture
```

```
});

var labelLocale = Titanium.UI.createLabel({
    width:  'auto',
    height: 30,
    top: 160,
    left: 10,
    font: {fontSize: 14, fontFamily: 'Helvetica'},
    color: '#000',
    text: 'Locale: ' + Titanium.Platform.locale
});

var labelModel = Titanium.UI.createLabel({
    width:  'auto',
    height: 30,
    top: 200,
    left: 10,
    font: {fontSize: 14, fontFamily: 'Helvetica'},
    color: '#000',
    text: 'Model: ' + Titanium.Platform.model
});


win1.add(labelOS);
win1.add(labelBattery);
win1.add(labelMemory);
win1.add(labelArchitecture);
win1.add(labelLocale);
win1.add(labelModel);
```

How it works...

Each of the labels in this code sample represents a different piece of information about your device and its capabilities. There is nothing particularly complicated about the code here but it's the methods themselves that are important.

Most of these are pretty self-explanatory. The methods for Battery, Memory, Architecture, and Model all provide you with information about the device and its specific capabilities. You may use these at certain times during your application's lifecycle, for instance, auto-saving data on a form when the battery reaches a certain critical level.

The most useful of all of these methods is `Titanium.Platform.osname`. It is this method that you will use constantly throughout the development of a Titanium cross-platform app as you will use it to check whether you're on iPhone or the Android platform, as seen in the following screenshot, and run certain code depending on that result.

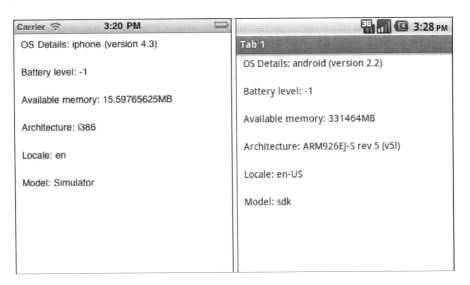

Obtaining the device's screen dimensions

While we developers are currently very lucky with the iPhone platform and its single resolution of 320x480 pixels, the same can't be said for Android. It is the Android platform in particular that, due to the way it's distributed among many manufacturers, has a number of differing screen ratios and resolutions. It is inevitable that there will be times where you may need to calculate the position of an object depending on the size of the current screen, without constantly resorting to a series of `Titanium.Platform.osname` checks.

Since the introduction of the iPhone 4, all new iOS devices have a retina display. Essentially, the screen resolution is still at 320x480 but the DPI is doubled, meaning the effective resolution is actually 640x960. Implementing for both these resolutions is very easy. Simply name all of your image files as normal, and then all of the double resolution files are named in the same way with the addition of an `@2x` flag. So if you had an image called `header.png`, which is designed for 320x480, you can create an image of double the size and name it `header@2x.png` and this will automatically be picked up by all iOS retina displays.

In this recipe, we will generate three views, one that takes up the bottom half of the screen, and another two that take up only the top. We'll do this using the `Titanium.Platform.displayCaps` functions.

The complete source code for this recipe can be found in the `/Chapter 11/Recipe 2` folder.

How to do it...

In your `app.js` file, we are going to create three different views, each taking up a separate portion of the screen. Remove any existing code and type in the following:

```
//
// create root window
//
var win1 = Titanium.UI.createWindow({
    title:'Tab 1',
    backgroundColor:'#fff'
});

var windowWidth = Titanium.Platform.displayCaps.platformWidth;
var windowHeight = Titanium.Platform.displayCaps.platformHeight;

var viewBottom = Titanium.UI.createView({
    width: windowWidth,
    height: windowHeight / 2,
    bottom: 0,
    left: 0,
    backgroundColor: 'Red'
});
win1.add(viewBottom);

var lblDeviceDPI = Titanium.UI.createLabel({
    text: 'The device DPI = ' +
  Titanium.Platform.displayCaps.dpi,
    width: windowWidth,
    height: windowHeight / 2,
    textAlign: 'center',
    bottom: 0,
    color: '#fff'
});
viewBottom.add(lblDeviceDPI);

var viewTop1 = Titanium.UI.createView({
    width: windowWidth / 2,
    height: windowHeight / 2,
    top: 0,
    left: 0,
    backgroundColor: 'Green'
});
win1.add(viewTop1);

var viewTop2 = Titanium.UI.createView({
```

```
        width: windowWidth / 2,
        height: windowHeight / 2,
        top: 0,
        left:  windowWidth / 2,
        backgroundColor: 'Blue'
});
win1.add(viewTop2);

//open root window
win1.open();
```

How it works...

The code here is pretty straightforward. Put simply, we are assigning the width and height values of the device to the two variables called `windowWidth` and `windowHeight`. To do this, we are using two of the properties available to us in the `Titanium.Platform.displayCaps` namespace; namely `platformWidth` and `platformHeight`. Once we have these values it's easy to then create our views and lay them out using some very simple calculations.

The following is an example of the same screen being rendered in two very different resolutions on both the iPhone and Android:

Understanding device orientation modes

One of the great benefits to users with current smartphones is the ability to hold the device in any way possible and have the screen rotate to suit its orientation. Titanium allows you to fire event handlers based on orientation changes in your application.

In this recipe, we will create an event handler that fires whenever the orientation on the device is changed, and we will re-arrange some UI components on our screen accordingly.

 The complete source code for this recipe can be found in the `/Chapter 11/Recipe 3` folder.

How to do it...

Open your `app.js` file, remove any existing code, and type in the following:

```
//
// create root window
//
var win1 = Titanium.UI.createWindow({
    title:'Tab 1',
    backgroundColor:'#fff'
});

//set the allowed orientation modes for win1
//in this example, we'll say ALL modes are allowed
win1.orientationModes = [
    Titanium.UI.LANDSCAPE_LEFT,
    Titanium.UI.LANDSCAPE_RIGHT,
    Titanium.UI.PORTRAIT,
    Titanium.UI.UPSIDE_PORTRAIT
];

var view1 = Titanium.UI.createView({
    width: Titanium.Platform.displayCaps.platformWidth,
    height: Titanium.Platform.displayCaps.platformHeight,
    backgroundColor: 'Blue'
});

var labelOrientation = Titanium.UI.createLabel({
    text: 'Currently in ? mode',
    width: '100%',
    textAlign: 'center',
    height: 30,
    color: '#000'
});
view1.add(labelOrientation);
win1.add(view1);
```

```
Ti.Gesture.addEventListener('orientationchange', function(e) {
    //check for landscape modes
    if (e.orientation == Titanium.UI.LANDSCAPE_LEFT ||
        e.orientation == Titanium.UI.LANDSCAPE_RIGHT) {
        view1.width =
         Titanium.Platform.displayCaps.platformWidth;
        view1.height =
         Titanium.Platform.displayCaps.platformHeight;
        labelOrientation.text = 'Currently in LANDSCAPE mode';
        view1.backgroundColor = 'Blue';
    }
    else {
        //we must be in portrait mode!
        view1.width =
         Titanium.Platform.displayCaps.platformWidth;
        view1.height =
         Titanium.Platform.displayCaps.platformHeight;
        labelOrientation.text = 'Currently in PORTRAIT mode';
        view1.backgroundColor = 'Yellow';
    }
});

//open root window
win1.open();
```

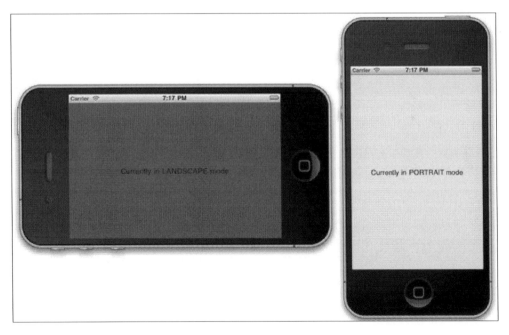

Try running your app now in the emulator or on your device, and orientating the screen between landscape and potrait modes. You should see changes like those in the previous screenshot!

How it works...

We are attaching an event listener into the `Ti.Gesture` and once the orientation of the device changes this event handler is fired and we can re-arrange the components on the screen as we see fit. Technically, we can really do anything we want within this handler. A great example might be having a `TableView` whilst in portrait mode and opening a new window containing a `MapView` when the user orientates the screen into landscape mode. Here we are simply changing both the colour of our main view object and the text property of the label contained within it in order to highlight the changes in the device orientation.

Coding around differences between the iOS and Android APIs

Although Appcelerator Titanium makes much of the hard work of integrating with numerous operating systems and devices invisible to you, the developer, there are going to be times when you simply have to write some code that is platform specific. The most common way to do this is by checking the `osname` property from the `Titanium.Platform` namespace.

In this recipe we will create a simple screen the shows a custom activity indicator when the device is an iPhone, and a standard indicator when the user is on an Android device.

 The complete source code for this recipe can be found in the `/Chapter 11/Recipe 4` folder.

How to do it...

Open your `app.js` file, remove any existing code, and type in the following:

```
// create root window
var win1 = Titanium.UI.createWindow({
    title: 'Tab 1',
    backgroundColor: '#fff'
});

///this next bit is a custom activity indicator for iphone
///due to too many diffs between android and ios ones
var actIndIphone = Titanium.UI.createView({
    width: 320,
    height: 480,
    backgroundColor: '#000',
    opacity: 0.75,
    visible: false
});
```

```
var actIndBg = Titanium.UI.createView({
    width: 280,
    height: 50,
    backgroundColor: '#000',
    opacity: 1,
    borderRadius: 5
});
var indicatorIphone = Titanium.UI.createActivityIndicator({
    width: 30,
    height: 30,
    left: 10,
    top: 10,
    color: '#fff',
    style: 1
});
actIndBg.add(indicatorIphone);

var actIndLabel = Titanium.UI.createLabel({
    left: 50,
    width: 220,
    height: 'auto',
    textAlign: 'left',
    text: 'Please wait, loading iPhone...',
    color: '#fff',
    font: {fontSize: 12, fontFamily: 'Helvetica'}
});
actIndBg.add(actIndLabel);
actIndIphone.add(actIndBg);
win1.add(actIndIphone);

//the important bit!
//check if platform is android and if so, show a normal dialog
//else show our custom iPhone one
if(Ti.Platform.osname == 'android')
{
    var indicatorAndroid = Titanium.UI.createActivityIndicator({
        title: 'Loading',
        message: 'Please wait, loading Android...'
    });
    indicatorAndroid.show();
}
else
{
```

```
        actIndIphone.visible = true;
        indicatorIphone.show();
    }


    //open root window
    win1.open();
```

Now run your application in both the Android and iPhone simulators. You should be able to tell that the code we wrote has recognized which platform you're running and is displaying an activity indicator differently on each.

How it works...

This simple recipe shows you how to code around differences in the two platforms using the simplest of "if" statements, namely by checking the osname of the current device using the Titanium.Platform.osname property. We have put this check to good use by only displaying our custom activity indicator view when we're on an iPhone. On the Android platform, this is unnecessary as the activity indicator will appear as a modal view on screen above all others simply by using its ".show()" method.

You can use this property to check the platform whenever you need to display a separate UI component or integrate with a platform independent API. An example of this recipe running on each device is shown in the following screenshot:

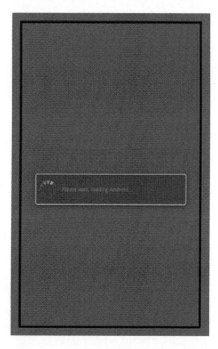

Ensuring your device can make phone calls

With all of the technical wizardry and touch-screen goodness that are now packed into modern day smartphones, it's easy to forget that their primary function is still that of a telephone which is capable of making and receiving voice calls. However, there may be times when the user's device is not capable of performing a call for whatever reason (poor network service, lack of call functionality that is iPod touch user, and so on).

In this recipe, we will attempt to make a phone call by first checking on the device's capabilities and throwing an error message when this is not possible.

 The complete source code for this recipe can be found in the `/Chapter 11/Recipe 5` folder.

How to do it...

Open your `app.js` file, remove any existing code, and type in the following:

```
// create root window
var win1 = Titanium.UI.createWindow({
    title: 'Tab 1',
    backgroundColor: '#fff'
});

//create the textfield number entry to dial
var txtNumber = Titanium.UI.createTextField({
    top: 20,
    left: 20,
    height: 40,
    width: 280,
    hintText: '+44 1234 321 231',
    borderStyle: 1
});
win1.add(txtNumber);

//create our call button
var btnCall = Titanium.UI.createButton({
    top: 90,
    left: 20,
    width: 280,
    height: 40,
    title: 'Call Now!'
});
```

```
//attempt a phone call
btnCall.addEventListener('click', function(e){
  if(txtNumber.value != '')
  {
      if(Titanium.Platform.osname != 'ipad'
      && Titanium.Platform.model != 'iPod Touch'
      && Titanium.Platform.model != 'google_sdk'
      && Titanium.Platform.model != 'Simulator')
      {
          Titanium.Platform.openURL('tel:' + txtNumber.value);
      }
      else
      {
          alert("Sorry, your device is not capable of making calls.");
      }
  }
  else
  {
      alert("You must provide a valid phone number!");
  }
});
win1.add(btnCall);


//open root window
win1.open();
```

Run your application now either in the simulator or on a device not capable of making calls, such as an iPod Touch. You should see an alert appear stating that the device can not action the requested phone call.

How it works...

Here we are simply using the Titanium Platform namespace to determine what kind of device the user is currently using, and providing an error message when that device is of the type iPod, iPad, or the emulator, as seen in the following screenshot. If the device in question is capable of making phone calls, such as the iPhone or an Android smartphone, then the device's phone API is called via means of a special URL request:

```
//must be a valid number, e.g. 'tel:07427555122'
Titanium.Platform.openURL('tel:' + txtNumber.value);
```

As long as the phone number being passed is valid, the device will launch the calling screen and attempt to place the call on the user's behalf.

12
Preparing your App for Distribution and Getting it Published

In this chapter, we will cover:

- ▶ Joining the iOS Developer Program
- ▶ Installing iOS Developer Certificates and Provisioning Profiles
- ▶ Build your app for iOS using Titanium Studio
- ▶ Joining the Google Android Developer Program
- ▶ Creating your application's distribution key
- ▶ Building and submitting your app to the Android Marketplace

Introduction

The final piece of our development puzzle is addressing how we package and distribute our Titanium applications to the iTunes store and Android Marketplace in order for our potential customers to download and enjoy all our hard work. Each of these stores has their own separate processes, certifications, and membership programs.

In this chapter, we'll show you how to set up your system in preparation for distribution and how to register for each site, as well as how to package and submit your apps to the iTunes and Android Marketplace stores.

Joining the iOS Developer Program

In order to submit applications to the iTunes store, you must first pay to become a member of the Apple's iOS Developer Program. Membership is paid, and starts from $99 USD (or equivalent), recurring annually. Even if you intend to develop and distribute your apps for free, you will still need to be a paid member of the iOS Developer Program. It is worth noting up front that only Mac users can follow and implement the steps for the iOS recipes since the building and distribution of iOS apps is only available to those running the Mac OSX operating system.

How to do it...

To register for Apple's iOS program, first open up a web browser and navigate to `http://developer.apple.com/programs/register`, and click on the **Get Started** link. The following page that loads will then ask you if you want to create a new Apple ID or use an existing one. Unless you have registered for some of Apple's developer services before, you should choose the **Create New Profile** link.

Once you are on the **Create Profile** page:

1. Provide your contact information, including your country of residence. This is important since you'll need to provide some evidence of your residence when you want to start selling paid applications.

2. On the next page, provide the information required in Professional Profile.

3. Finally, carefully read and agree to the Terms and Conditions set out by Apple and confirm that you agree, and are at least 18 years old (or the legal equivalent in your country). Click on the **I Agree** button to complete your account creation.

4. Apple will then send you an e-mail with a confirmation code/link. Clicking on this link in your e-mail will open your browser and confirm your e-mail address and complete your account setup.

You should now be able to see the following page in your browser. It is from here that we will register to the Developer Program and pay the $99 USD (or equivalent) annual fee.

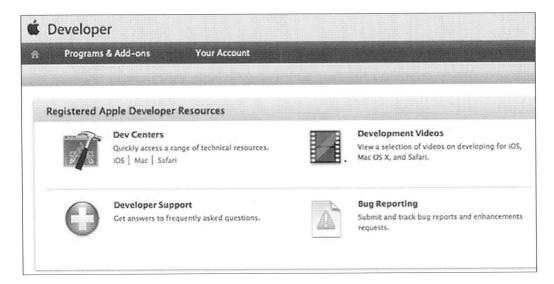

Click on the **Programs & Add-ons** tab in the top left of the page's menu, which will take you to a page showing the list of memberships you are currently subscribed to. Presuming you have a new account, then a list of three developer programs should appear, each with a **Join Today** button on the right. To continue, follow these steps:

1. Click on the iOS Developer Program's **Join Today** button, which should appear at the top of that list.

2. On the next page that loads, click on **Enroll Now**, and continue until you get to the step-by-step wizard.

3. Select **I'm registered as a developer with Apple and would like to enroll in a paid Apple Developer Program**. from the list on the right and press **Continue**.

4. From here you need to provide all of the information asked of you in order to complete your account setup. You should choose whether to register as a business or individual. Be aware that whichever method of registration you should choose you need to ensure you have all of the relevant documentation. You will be asked to submit this documentation for verification by Apple and you'll not be able to submit paid applications until that documentation is received and approved. Some of this information cannot be changed and once you have entered it and completed the application it is, for all intents and purposes, set in stone!

5. Finally, agree to the final set of terms and conditions and then make your payment online. You will require a credit card or debit card to make this purchase.

You should now be able to log in to your new Apple Developer account by navigating your browser to `http://developer.apple.com/devcenter/ios`. Once logged in, you should get some new menu options on your account's home page, including **Provisioning** and **iTunes Connect**. Any information you are missing for your account can be found under the iTunes Connect option, under the **Contracts, Tax and Banking** section. It is likely that you may need to upload some documentation and agree to new terms and conditions from time to time within this section of the website.

Installing iOS Developer Certificates and Provisioning Profiles

There are two types of certificates required to build your applications, both for debugging on a device and for iTunes store distribution. The first is your Development Certificate. This certificate is installed on your Mac within the `KeyChain` and is used for every single application you will develop. It identifies you, the developer, when you are distributing an app.

The second type is the application's Provisioning Profile. This profile certificate is both application specific and release specific. This means you'll need to create a separate profile for each state of the application you wish to release (most commonly being Development and Distribution).

In this recipe, we will go through the process of creating and installing your Developer Certificate, and then creating and using an application-specific Provisioning Profile in Titanium Studio.

How to do it...

We will now start off with the steps required for installing iOS Developer Certificates and Provisioning Profiles.

1. Set up your iOS Developer Certificate.

2. Log in to your Apple Developer account if you have not done so already, at `http://developer.apple.com/ios`, and click on the **iOS Provisioning Portal** link. The page that loads will have a number of options on the left-hand menu, click on the **Certificates** option. A page will load with a series of steps entitled **How to create a Development Certificate**. You will need to follow these steps exactly as described, and when you have gone through them from start to finish you should have a Certificate Signing Request (CSR) file saved on your Mac. For this recipe, we'll make the assumption that you have followed these steps closely and have saved a CSR to your desktop.

3. Click on the **Choose** button at the bottom of the screen to select the CSR file from your computer and upload it to the web page. Once it has finished uploading, select the **Submit** button in the bottom right corner of the page.

   When the screen reloads, you should now see a certificate appear in the grid, with the name you gave it when generated, and a status of **Pending Issuance**. If you own the iOS account, you can simply wait 20-30 seconds and refresh the page to have the status change to **Issued** and a **Download** action appear to the right of the grid. If the account you are using belongs to another party, you will need to wait for them to confirm this action before you receive an issued certificate. Download the certificate now, and double-click the resulting saved file when it has completed downloading. It will then automatically open in `KeyChain` Access and show you that it's been installed. If you have a message at the bottom of the page about the WWDR certificate needing to be installed, you may also choose to download and run that at this point.

4. Setting up your device.

   If you have an iPhone or iPod touch and wish to test with it, then you first need to register that device against your iTunes account. Click on the **Devices** menu link on the left-hand side of the page and then **Add Device**. The screen that appears will ask you for information about who owns the device, and more specifically, what that device's unique identifier is. You can find this identifier by plugging in your device to your Mac and opening iTunes. It will appear under **My iPhone/iPod** and then clicking on the **Serial Number** label that appears.

An example of the unique identifier is shown in the following screenshot:

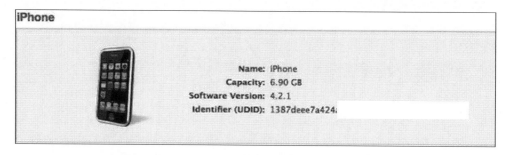

5. Creating your Application Provisioning profile.

   Now that your Developer Certificate is set up, it's time to create the provisioning profiles for an application we have built. For this example, we're going to use the details for the **LoanCalc** app we built in *Chapter 1*. However, you could use any application you have already created.

Click on the **App IDs** link from the left-hand menu, and when the screen loads, select the **New App ID** button.

Give your app a description and leave the Bundle Seed ID drop down list set as **Generate New**.

Enter in the Bundle Identifier. This is the all-important identifier that you give your application upon its creation in Titanium Studio. In this example, our bundle identifier is com.packtpub.loancalc.

Press **Submit** to complete the process and generate your App ID.

Now click on **Provisioning** and select **New Profile** after the screen loads. It should have the **Development** tab activated.

Choose a name for your profile. We'll keep it simple and call this one **LoanCalc Development Profile**. You should now be able to check your certificate checkbox, and choose the LoanCalc app identifier from the drop down list, as well as the device you wish to use for this Development profile. Press **Submit** when you have completed filling in the form.

Your new profile should now appear in the list of profiles under the **Development** tab. Wait for 20-30 seconds and refresh the page, and its status should change from **Pending** to **Download**. Download the certificate to a location on your computer such as the Desktop.

Repeat the previous steps, but instead of choosing the **Development** tab options, choose the **Distribution** tab instead. You'll also have an additional option when creating the certificate for **Distribution: App Store or Ad Hoc**. If you want to distribute your app on the iTunes store, ensure you check the first radio button option.

> If you're not the account owner, but have been given membership status to someone else's iTunes account (e.g. if you are the employee of a larger company), then you need to ensure that you've been given admin access in order to set up your certificates and profiles.

Build your app for iOS using Titanium Studio

In this recipe, we will continue the process started in the two recipes prior to this one and build our application for both development and distribution to the iTunes store.

> Remember, if all else fails, you can always build your application manually in XCode by navigating to the `build/iphone` folder of your project and opening the XCode project file.

How to do it...

1. Building your application for development.

    i. Open your project in Titanium Studio; we are using the `LoanCalc` app from *Chapter 1* as an example, however, you may use any project you wish. Ensure that the Application ID in Titanium Studio (on the **Edit** tab) matches the ID you used when creating your provisioning profiles. In our case, this ID is `com.packtpub.loancalc`.

    ii. Switch across to the **Test & Package** tab, and choose **Run on Device**. Titanium Studio should automatically have the iPhone option highlighted. If it doesn't, then you either aren't on a Mac (required) or perhaps don't have the necessary XCode tools installed. You can download XCode from `http://developer.apple.com/xcode`.

iii. On the file selection icon next to the **Upload Provisioning Profile** text box, select the development profile you created for LoanCalc. Presuming you installed your **WWDR** Certificate and Development Certificate properly as per the previous recipe, you should now see a screen similar to the one shown in the following screenshot:

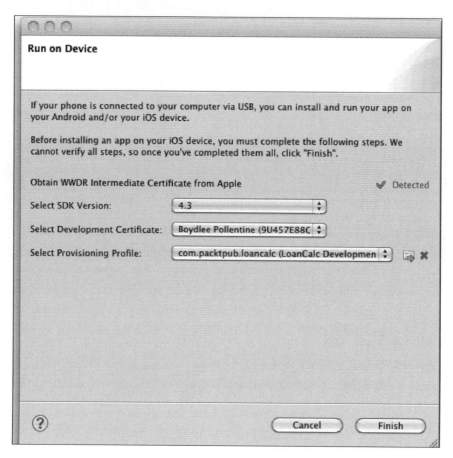

iv. Press the **Finish** button to have Titanium Studio kick off the build process. During this process your application will be built and added to your list of apps in the iTunes library. You will need to sync your iPhone or iPod Touch in order to get your app running on your device.

2. Building your applications for distribution.

    i. First, we need to create your new application in iTunes Connect, on the Apple
        Developer website. Navigate to the iTunes Connect section on the Apple
        Developer website in your browser and click **Manage Applications**. The
        next screen that loads will list all of your current apps (if you have created
        any). To create a new one, click **Add New App** in the top left corner. Add in
        the information requested, including the app name (**Packt LoanCalc** in our
        example) and select the LoanCalc app from the product identifier list. The
        SKU can be any code you wish, e.g. packtpub001. Fill in the information on
        the next two screens with a description, keywords, screenshots, and data
        about your application. When finished, you should be forwarded to a screen
        that looks like the one shown:

    ii. Now, if you're ready to upload, press the **View Details** button in the bottom
         left, and on the next page that loads, press the **Ready To Upload Binary**
         button that appears in the top right of the screen. Apple will ask you a couple
         of security questions. Answer these and your App status will changed from
         Prepare for Upload to **Ready for Upload**.

    iii. Switch back to Titanium`Studio, make sure your project is selected in the
          Project explorer page, and then select the **Distribution** button followed by
          the **Distribute – App Store** option.

iv. You should now be faced with a similar screen to the one you used to package your app for development testing. Enter in a distribution location (any will do, we have chosen the `Downloads` folder for this example), and choose your Distribution profile that you saved from the previous recipe. Your **Distribute** screen in Titanium Studio should now look something like this:

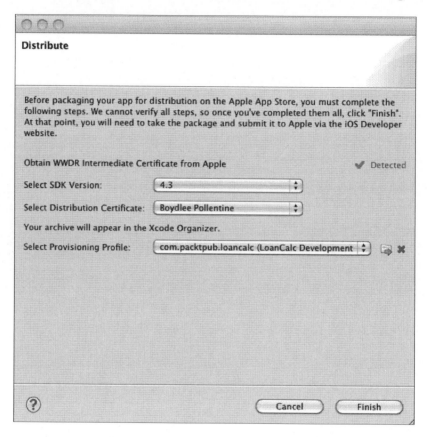

v. Hit the **Finish** button to start the build process. If you get an error about a missing file in the `Users/ [your username] /Library/MobileDevice/ Provisioning Profiles` directory, then simply copy the Distribution profile saved on your computer to this directory and rename it to the name of the missing file in the error dialog.

vi. When this process is complete, XCode should load and the Organizer window should appear on screen with your application archived and ready to be submitted to the iTunes store, as seen in the following screenshot:

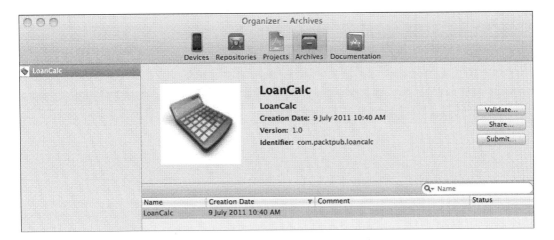

vii. Hit **Submit** on this screen and follow the prompts. If everything has been done correctly (and according to Apple's rules), your app should be uploaded to the iTunes server and you should receive email confirmation of it being received within a few minutes!

You can check on the progress of your submission at any time via the iTunes Connect section of the developer program website. Approval usually takes between 1-2 weeks. However, this tends to fluctuate depending on the number of submissions and whether your app is rejected or requires changes before approval will be granted. Apple will send you emails at each stage of the submission cycle, including when you first submit the app, when they start reviewing it, and when they approve or reject it.

Joining the Google Android Developer Program

In order to submit applications to the Android Marketplace, you must first register a Google account, and then register for both a Google Checkout account and Android Developer account. All of these accounts utilize the same username and password combination and the process is quite straightforward. Membership is paid, and starts from $25 USD (or equivalent), and is a one-time payment.

How to do it...

To register, first open up a web browser and navigate to `http://market.android.com/publish`. You'll be asked to log in to your Google Account (as seen in the following screenshot). If you don't have one, then this is the stage at which you need to create an account.

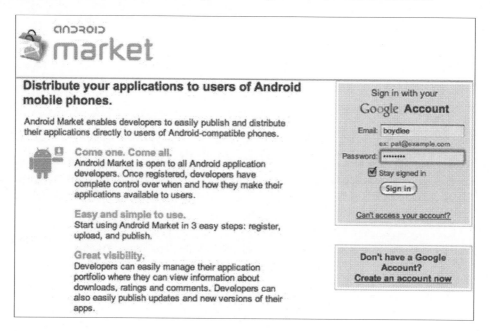

Once you've completed the sign in or registration process, you'll then be asked to provide your Developer/Publisher details. After that, you'll be required to pay the US $25 registration fee. That's it—simple and straightforward! You can now start to create and upload applications to the Android Marketplace.

 Google may send you an e-mail a few weeks after registering, asking for identification for the account, usually in the form of a passport or driver's licence. You can e-mail them this information back within the allotted timeframe and all will be well.

Creating your application's distribution key

In order to build applications made for the Android Marketplace, you need to create a distribution key on your local computer. This key is used to digitally sign your app.

How to do it...

Open the Terminal if you use Mac or Linux, or alternatively the command prompt if you're a Windows user. Change the current directory to the following using the `cd` command:

```
cd /<path to your android sdk>/tools
//e.g. cd /Users/boydlee/android-sdk/tools
```

To create the key, we need to use the Java **keytool** located in this directory. In the command prompt/terminal, type in the following, while replacing `my-release-key.keystore` and `alias_name` with the key and alias of your application:

```
Windows: START»Command
$ keytool -genkey -v -keystore my-release-key.keystore -alias alias_name
-keyalg RSA -validity 10000

Windows: Mac: Terminal
$ keytool -genkey -v -keystore my-release-key.keystore -alias alias_name
-keyalg RSA -validity 10000
```

For example, our `LoanCalc` application key command will look something like:

```
$ keytool -genkey -v -keystore packtpub.loancalc -alias loancalc -keyalg
RSA -validity 10000
```

Press *Enter* and execute the command and you'll be asked a series of questions. You need to provide a password for the keystore - it would be wise to write it down as you will need it to package your app later. We'll use the password `packtpub`. When you are prompted for the secondary key password, simply press *Enter* to use the same one.

Now your key will be exported and saved to the directory you were currently in. In our case, this is the `tools` directory under our Android SDK folder. You will need to remember the file location in order to build your Android app using Titanium Studio in the next recipe.

Building and submitting your app to the Android Marketplace

In this recipe, we will continue the process started in the two previous recipes and build our application for distribution to the Android Marketplace.

How to do it...

Open your project in Titanium Studio. We are using the `LoanCalc` app from *Chapter 1* as an example, however, you may use any project you wish. Make sure your project is selected in the Project explorer page, and then select the **Distribution** button followed by the **Distribute – Android** option, as seen in the following screenshot:

You will need to enter in the distribution location (where you want the packaged APK file saved to) and the location of the keystore file you created in the previous recipe, along with the password and alias you provided earlier. After you enter in that information it should look something like the following screenshot:

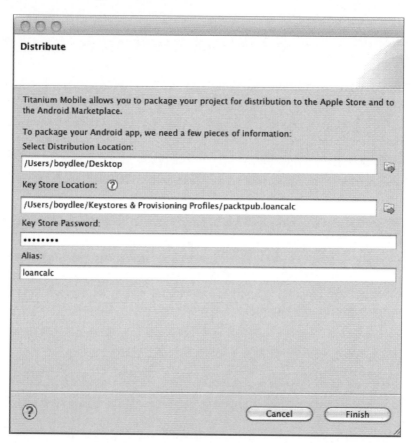

If all of the information is correct, click **Finish**. After a few minutes the APK file will be written out to the distribution location you provided. Go back to the Android Marketplace website, and on the home screen, click **Add New Application**. Select the **Upload** button and choose your saved APK (LoanCalc.apk in our case) and upload it to the server. If everything was successful, you should see a screen similar to the one shown next:

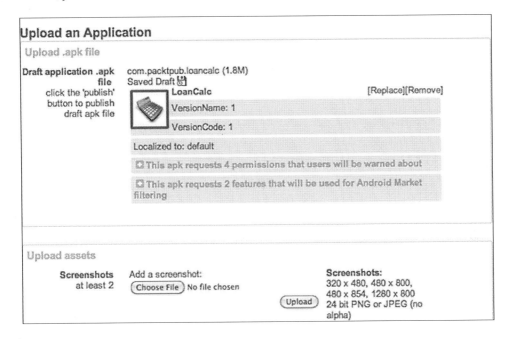

All that is left to do now is fill in the remaining information, including a description and title for your app, plus some screenshots. You will also be asked to select pricing information and agree to Google's terms and conditions. Once that is done, all that is left to do is press **Submit**. Within a few minutes, your application should start to appear in the Android Marketplace! Unlike Apple, there is no approval process necessary for apps submitted for Android.

You should now be able to build and submit applications to both the Apple and Android Marketplaces.

Index

B

background service
creating, on iPhone 196, 197
Base64 encoding 206
basic authentication
about 206
used, for accessing Blurtit API 206-209
bccRecipients method 137
Birdhouse
tweet, sending through 153, 154
blur() method 226
Blurtit 206
Blurtit API
accessing, basic authentication used 206-209
URL 206
btnGetPhoto object 112
btnSaveCurrentPhoto click event 128
btnSave object 182
buttonEmail object 136
buttons
creating 29-32
buttonStyle property 239

C

callMethod() function 222
camera
photos, capturing from 102-105
cancel event 105
cancel property 101
capture device
selecting, OptionDialog used 98-102
captured photo
saving, to device file system 111-113
ccRecipients method 137
cd command 281
Certificate Signing Request (CSR) 273
chartHTML 37
Charting library
URL, for downloading 36
charts
about 36
creating, Raphael JS used 36-38
check-in
posting, to FourSquare 220-222
click event 31

click event listener 175
click events
capturing 29-32
clipboard
about 193
data, retrieving via 193-195
data, storing via 193-195
close() method 12
contacts address book
accessing 189-192
contentOffset property 70
CREATE 42
createDirectory() method 113
createEmailDialog() method 136
create keyword 12
createOptionDialog() method 101
createPerson method 192
createScrollableView() method 110
currentPage property 110
current position
retrieving, GeoLocation used 78-80
custom events
used, for passing event data between app and Webview 163-166
custom Facebook application
setting up 140, 141
custom rows
used, for enhancing TableViews 48-50
custom variables
passing, between windows 28, 29

D

Dashcode 9
data
displaying, TableView used 45-47
fetching, from Google Places API 209-213
reading, from remote XML through HTTPClient 42-44
retrieving, from SQLite database 64-67
retrieving, via clipboard 193-195
retrieving, via Yahoo YQL 223-226
saving, SQLite database used 59-61
searching, via Yahoo YQL 223-226
storing, via clipboard 193-195
data array object 47
database.js file 59

R

Raphael
 about 38
 URL, for documentation 39
Raphael JS
 used, for creating charts 36-38
Raphael JS library
 URL, for downloading 36
Recipe Finder app 67
recordCurrentLocation() method 92
regionFit property 77
region property 77
remote data access
 speeding up, Yahoo YQL and JSON used 54-57
remote XML
 data, reading from 42-44
rename() method 129
request header 213
Resources directory 36
resultSet method 64, 66
resultSet.close() method 66
resultSet.next() method 66
routes
 drawing, on MapView 89-92
RSS feeds
 about 132
 combining 58

S

sale
 modules, packaging for 251, 252
saved files
 deleting, from file system 127-130
save to photos option 108
screen dimension
 obtaining, for device 257-259
ScrollableView
 about 108
 used, for displaying photos 109, 110
SearchBar component
 about 51
 used, for filtering TableView 51-53
searchYQL() function 226
SELECT 42
SelectedPerson function 192

SelectedProperty function 192
send() method 44, 207
setChosenImage function 175
setInterval() method 92
setText() method 195
showCamera() method 102, 105
showContacts() method 192
show() method 34
Slider control
 used, for scaling ImageView 180, 181
Sliders
 about 24
 Titanium applications , enhancing with 25-27
SQL
 reference link 42
SQLite 183
SQLite database
 creating 58, 59
 creating ways 58
 data, retrieving from 64-66
 pre-populated database file, attaching 59
 used, for saving data 59-62
SQLite Database Browser tool 59
SQL statements
 CREATE 42
 DELETE 42
 INSERT 42
 SELECT 42
Structured Query Language. *See* **SQL**
subject parameter 136
success event 105
Switches
 about 24
 Titanium applications , enhancing with 25-27

T

TabGroup
 about 12
 adding, to Titanium applications 12-15
TableRow objects
 creating 48-50
TableView
 about 45
 enhancing, with custom rows 48-50
 filtering, SearchBar component used 51-53
 used, for displaying data 45-47

Thank you for buying
Appcelerator Titanium Smartphone App Development Cookbook

About Packt Publishing

Packt, pronounced 'packed', published its first book "*Mastering phpMyAdmin for Effective MySQL Management*" in April 2004 and subsequently continued to specialize in publishing highly focused books on specific technologies and solutions.

Our books and publications share the experiences of your fellow IT professionals in adapting and customizing today's systems, applications, and frameworks. Our solution based books give you the knowledge and power to customize the software and technologies you're using to get the job done. Packt books are more specific and less general than the IT books you have seen in the past. Our unique business model allows us to bring you more focused information, giving you more of what you need to know, and less of what you don't.

Packt is a modern, yet unique publishing company, which focuses on producing quality, cutting-edge books for communities of developers, administrators, and newbies alike. For more information, please visit our website: www.packtpub.com.

Writing for Packt

We welcome all inquiries from people who are interested in authoring. Book proposals should be sent to author@packtpub.com. If your book idea is still at an early stage and you would like to discuss it first before writing a formal book proposal, contact us; one of our commissioning editors will get in touch with you.

We're not just looking for published authors; if you have strong technical skills but no writing experience, our experienced editors can help you develop a writing career, or simply get some additional reward for your expertise.

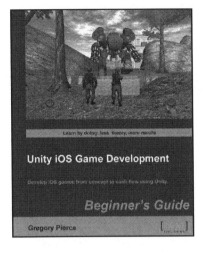

Unity iOS Game Development Beginners Guide

ISBN: 978-1-84969-040-9   Paperback: 432 pages

Develop iOS games from concept to cash flow using Unity

1. Dive straight into game development with no previous Unity or iOS experience

2. Work through the entire lifecycle of developing games for iOS

3. Add multiplayer, input controls, debugging, in app and micro payments to your game

4. Implement the different business models that will enable you to make money on iOS games

Xcode 4 iOS Development Beginner's Guide

ISBN: 978-1-84969-130-7   Paperback: 432 pages

Use the powerful Xcode 4 suite of tools to build applications for the iPhone and iPad from scratch

1. Learn how to use Xcode 4 to build simple, yet powerful applications with ease

2. Each chapter builds on what you have learned already

3. Learn to add audio and video playback to your applications

4. Plentiful step-by-step examples, images, and diagrams to get you up to speed in no time with helpful hints along the way

Please check **www.PacktPub.com** for information on our titles

Printed in Great Britain
by Amazon.co.uk, Ltd.,
Marston Gate.